G. Simon Harak, S.J.

VIRTUOUS PASSIONS:
The Formation of Christian Character

PAULIST PRESS
New York/Mahwah

Library of Congress Cataloging-in-Publication Data

Harak, G. Simon, 1948-
    Virtuous passions: the formation of Christian character/G. Simon Harak.
        p.   cm.
    Includes bibliographical references and index.
    ISBN 0-8091-3436-5 (pbk.)
    1 Christian ethics—Catholic authors. 2. Emotions—Religious aspects—Catholic Church. 3. Catholic Church—Doctrines. 4. Thomas, Aquinas, Saint, 1225?-1274. 5. Ignatius, of Loyola, Saint, 1491-1556. I. Title.
B1249.H3575   1993
241—dc20   93-23503
                                                                              CIP

Published by Paulist Press
997 Macarthur Boulevard
Mahwah, NJ 07430

Printed and bound in the United States of America

CONTENTS

Dedication

To the memory of Raymond Bertrand, S.J.
and to
Terê Dalumpines
with gratitude and love

ACKNOWLEDGMENTS

I have come to discover, in the course of writing this book, how much authorship is an experience of shared passion in community. My discovery of the passions really began when I participated in St. Ignatius' *Spiritual Exercises* under the direction of Raymond Bertrand, S.J. in January 1971. Stanley Hauerwas first encouraged my academic interest in the passions and in Aquinas' *Treatise*. Rev. David Burrell, C.S.C. at the University of Notre Dame patiently oversaw and reviewed my earliest writing on the topic. Betsy Hoagg and the library staff at Fairfield University helped me with my research for this book, as did the entire UND library staff. John Thiel, the Chair of my Department of Religious Studies at Fairfield, was always willing and able to give me insightful criticism on my work, and I cannot imagine a more supportive group of colleagues than the members of my department. Anthony Serianni of UND made sure the science in Chapter 1 was "basically correct." James Long of Fairfield's Department of Philosophy helped me especially with Chapter 3. Howard Gray, S.J. kindly assisted me with Chapter 5. My nonviolent community helped me with Chapter 6, as have all who have taught and shared with me the struggle for justice. These all offered their encouragement as well as their wisdom.

The entire book was read (and reread, and reread) by my brother, Philip Harak, and my friends Katherine Doolittle, Robert Doolittle and Carolyn Rusiackas. If the reader finds any part of my writing elegant, it is due to their insistence on clarity, and their sharing with me the joy of this project. Dick Sparks, C.S.P. at Paulist Press kept up his enthusiasm for this project for the two years that I was working on it. Finally, I have several times taught a course called "The Passions and the Virtues" to students who have laughed, wept, and loved God together with me. It is their voices and faces that I kept before me as I wrote.

PREFACE: BEING MOVED

Moved with compassion, Jesus stretched out his hand,
touched him and said to him, "I am willing. Be healed."
—Mk 1:41

We were in Kingston, Jamaica, at a home for boys who were
orphaned or from abusive homes. It was the first day that the "big
brothers" (18-19 years old) from St. George's College had come to be
introduced to their new "little brothers." They had all been playing soccer when Fabian, the elected leader of the young men from St.
George's, came to me distraught and upset. His little brother, with
whom he was trying so hard to get along, had scored a goal in the
game. Everyone was excited. Fabian ran up to him and lifted his hand
to clap him on the shoulder. But the young boy flinched, and then cow-
ered away from him. Fabian was stunned. "I was going to congratulate
him," he kept saying to me. "I wasn't going to hurt him. What did he
pull away for? I wasn't going to hurt him."

It was a while before Fabian could reflect with me on what had
happened. And when he did, he discovered what must have been the
truth: that every time someone had raised a hand to that little boy, he
had been struck. Now, even when a hand was raised in congratulation,
the boy had no choice. I watched the expression on Fabian's face
change, and then he loped silently back to the field.

Later, on the way home, Fabian tentatively volunteered something to me. "I felt something," he said, and I paused. "Can you say
what it was?" I asked. Now Jamaica is a slow place, and we must have

1

walked five minutes in the heat and the mosquitoes before Fabian replied. "Moved," he said. "I felt moved."

This book is about being moved—about passions. I will keep coming back to the story I just told, because it seems to me that Fabian experienced passion in a primal sense on that day. Like Fabian, we experience ourselves being "moved," being affected in many ways in our own lives. We find ourselves seized by fear, stricken by jealousy, falling in love, surprised by joy, moved with compassion. The other seems to grasp us, to move us, sometimes even to compel our worship.

When I refer in this book to our common experience of being moved by, or moving the other, I will use the general term "affectivity." When I use the word "other," I am referring in general to all persons, events, and things beyond ourselves which affect us, which move us somehow. And because this is a study of ethics, I want to begin now by asking: Can we be morally responsible for the way we are moved? Can our passions be morally praise- or blameworthy? At first glance, the answer to those questions would seem to be "no"; we cannot be responsible for how an other affects us. We are responsible for our actions, we are told, not for our passions. And we often hear that judgment affirmed in the popular, "Your feelings are not good or bad, they're just feelings." But if we reflect a moment, we find that our sense of passions is not neutral. It is somehow wrong not to feel revulsion at rape, or to stay forever angry with imperfect parents. It is somehow right to rejoice at a friend's success, or to be moved by the plight of an abused child. So it seems upon reflection that our passions can be morally praise- or blameworthy after all. It is my central concern in this book to work out a moral theological account of that sense of the rightness or wrongness of passions, and, further, to consider ways to transform morally blameworthy passions, and to foster morally praiseworthy passions.

That sense that there is a rightness and wrongness about passions is corroborated by a history of moral reflection that reaches back at least as far as Plato[1] and Aristotle. That tradition tells us that moral agents, persons who are morally responsible for their actions, are also morally responsible for their passions. For example, Aristotle tells us that his whole study of morality in the *Nicomachean Ethics* is "concerned with pleasure and pain, for it is not unimportant for our actions whether we feel joy and pain in the right or wrong way" (1105a7).[2] He then becomes even more specific. At the close of Book II, he writes, "[Virtue] is a mean in the sense that it aims at the median in passions and in actions.... Anyone can get angry—that is easy—or can give away money or spend it; but to do all this to the right person, to the right extent, at the right time, for the right reason, and in the right way is no longer something easy that anyone can do. It is for this reason that good conduct is rare, praiseworthy, and noble" (1109a23-29).[3]

According to Aristotle, then, virtue is concerned with pleasures and pains which "are a consequence of every passion and every action."[4] And specific virtues are concerned with specific passions. Courage, he says, is the virtue concerned with fear and confidence. Gentleness is concerned with anger, modesty with shame. In fact, we could say that the passions are the ground, the material, the "stuff" of virtue in our moral project, our learning to live moral lives. Learning virtue is not just learning how to act (how to "give away money" in Aristotle's example). It is learning how to be moved (angered, shamed, delighted, drawn) by the right persons and things, to the right extent, for the right reasons, in the right way, at the right time.

The passions have been a concern for ethicists throughout the history of moral reflection. Premodern writers almost always used the word "passions" in their discussions of how we are moved. Later, in modern discussions of affectivity, theorists began to distinguish between passions and emotions. Now few scientific researchers, philosophers or theologians use the word "passions" at all, employing instead the word "affectivity," or even just "emotions" to refer generically to the whole spectrum of affective interaction. In this work, however, I will use "passion" because in the affective give and take of relationships I want to concentrate on the ethical significance of the agent's being moved, and because I want to be true to our ethical heritage in discussing the passions.

This is also a work of virtue ethics. Virtue ethics offers the attractive insight that "morality is not something we create, but something by which we are claimed.... The emphasis now is not on values we create, but on values we discover, goods to which we submit...."[5] Contemporary virtue ethicists, heirs of Aristotle, consistently challenge the prevailing model of the moral agent as necessarily "autonomous," that is, free from outside influences in her decisions or actions. Instead they offer a welcome stress on the social and even on the worshipful nature of our moral project. Such convictions would certainly seem to dispose them toward consideration of the experience of being moved. And yet contemporary virtue ethicists often lack a systematic treatment of the most common, most immediate and visceral experience of "being claimed"—the passions. They have concentrated more on action, rather than on passion, in their discussions of virtue. In so doing, they have not seriously challenged the prevailing moral attitude toward the passions: that the will or the intellect must *control* the passions. Nor have they seen that the uncritical acceptance of such a model weakens their own description of the moral project.

Meanwhile, there has been a veritable explosion of contemporary studies in the general area of affectivity,[6] but done mostly in the physical sciences: biochemistry and neurophysiology. Those studies are a good place to begin reclaiming our heritage of moral, theological reflection on the passions, because the passions are so unavoidably physical. One reason that moral theologians have difficulty with the passions may be that the body is such a "messy" category for moral reflection, especially if one is trying to talk about being an independent moral agent. For example, look at the quote from the gospel of Mark with which this preface begins. We often see the translation, "Moved with compassion," or "Moved with pity," or even "Feeling sorry for him...." But the Greek would probably best be translated, "It hit Jesus in his gut." A "messy" translation indeed! In fact, the whole pericope in Mark is inescapably physical in its tone. A leper—an "untouchable"—comes up to Jesus; he falls on his knees and pleads with Jesus; Jesus experiences a "gut-wrenching" compassion; he stretches out his hand; he touches the untouchable; he heals. And therein lies the ethical tale: from the perspective of our embodiment, we have needs that render us so dependent on the other—so open to passion—that it is almost impossible to impute to moral agents the autonomy that is so prized in the prevailing ethical model.

Thus if we are going to continue to enjoy the richness of the virtue ethicists' account of moral responsibility, and especially if we intend to be faithful to the incarnational aspects of Christian moral reflection, we need to attend to the moral agent first from the perspective of her embodiment. And that is where contemporary scientific studies on the passions become so useful for our project. In the first chapter, we will discuss the origin and persistence of the prevailing model of control of the passions. But then we will explore current scientific research to develop a more adequate account of affectivity. I want to discover: What happens to us biochemically, neurologically, when we become angry or afraid, delighted or joyful? And how might an awareness of those physical dimensions of passion affect our understanding of moral agency?

In the second chapter we will discuss contemporary philosophical and theological models of affectivity, keeping current scientific research in mind. We will emerge from that inquiry with a new model of the passions that will both fit the evidence of current research and preserve our ancestral understanding that we are morally responsible for how we are moved. And to make a bridge between past and current discussions, we will then place that new model in dialogue with two theologians who are ancestors in the tradition of moral reflection on the passions: Thomas Aquinas and Ignatius of Loyola. I think we will find them refreshingly current, and that this interchange between past and present reflections on passions will illuminate the thought of both contemporary and ancestor.[7] We will end with a chapter that will address a passion implicit in our first story of Fabian and his little brother, a passion for justice, and for an end to violence.

I hope, however, to discover something more in the course of this study. I hope to discover what Ignatius and Thomas are anxious to teach us: that we can be moved by our passions to communion with God's own self, and that all our passions can be ordered toward that goal. All our passions—from a passion for chocolate to a passion for justice—all of them caught up in the joy of the love of "the One who loved me and gave himself up for me"—caught up in a passion for God.

1.

THE BODY

The point of stressing biological facts is to suggest that our nature matters—that it defines our range of choice quite firmly, and must be understood if we are to give any meaning to the idea of freedom.... It only becomes a menace when it is made reductive and exclusive.
—Mary Midgley, *Heart and Mind*

We are, after all, talking about the event Christians call "incarnation," flesh-taking, before all else a bodily, material event.
—Rosemary Haughton, *The Passionate God*

I. Being Strong: The Prevailing Model

Those who think about the passions today are often puzzled about what to make of the bodily changes attributed to them. Premoderns, of course, had no such difficulty, since they did not posit a distinction between a passion and its embodiment.[1] Leonardo, for example, could instruct his students to paint a figure which "will have his hair standing on end, his eyebrows lowered and drawn together, and teeth clenched, with the two lateral corners of his mouth arched downwards. His neck will bulge and overlap in creases at the front as he stoops over his enemy."[2] And they would have succeeded in portraying *anger*.

Even up until the late seventeenth and early eighteenth centuries, common people identified the physical dimension of passion with the passion itself. In the courtship and betrothal customs of that period, the "people viewed love as something tangible, felt in the same way as we feel a blow, savor a taste, or sense a stare. Just as much as they feared the harm that could be transmitted by the evil eye, [they] reveled in the effects of a potion, a charm, the power of a lover's gaze, kiss, embrace, even a blow."[3] They were, in other words, conscious of being physically affected, touched, moved by passion.

In the meantime, seventeenth and eighteenth century academics were increasingly influenced by the philosophy of René Descartes. Descartes, writing in the mid-seventeenth century, was facing the Copernican-Galilean revolution, which made it impossible to trust the senses in the old way, for even seeing the sun move around the sky was seeing a falsity. Descartes struggled to find the most fundamental and reliable starting place from which to begin his philosophical analysis, and he found it in his own power to think. Even in doubting, Descartes could not doubt his rational ability to doubt. We know Descartes' "I think, therefore I am,"[4] so well because it so succinctly reveals his insight on what made humans human: their rationality.

Descartes' model of the rational moral agent fit a special ethical need for Enlightenment society in general, and for France in particular. His efforts were at least in part a reaction to the terrible feudalistic, nationalistic and religious controversies and bloodshed that had continuously plagued Europe.[5] The wish grew to find a place beyond, or outside of, those powerful influences, where one could go to determine the right and the wrong apart from community claims and emotional attachments which seemed to be clouding people's minds. Descartes fulfilled that wish by providing what Susan Bordo has called "the flight to objectivity," the creation of a new image of the ideal moral agent: an *observer* who would *objectively* examine *facts*, and then *evaluate* them.

Descartes is important in our study because he, more than any other thinker, articulated Enlightenment thinking about the passions, and is responsible for the present prevailing model of virtue as a struggle for control of the passions by reason. His position is so persuasive that all of us have undoubtedly found ourselves in our daily lives obeying "moral commands" based on Cartesian principles. "Don't get so emotional," someone cautions us, and we try to look at things "more rationally." "Let's look at this objectively," someone proposes, and we breathe a sigh of relief that we don't have to deal with messy emotions. But of course the presentation of the moral agent as a "rational observer of objective facts" is purely a theoretical construct. In reality, and especially in our embodied reality, we cannot be divorced from our own projects in our encounter with the other. As we will see, scientific studies reveal that our personal sense of what is worthwhile affects our perception of what is important, and even affects whether we perceive a thing at all.

Descartes' attempt to place an objective moral agent in the world falsely abstracts the moral agent from being in interaction with the other. When it came to applying his general philosophical principles to the passions, Descartes was forced to take a peculiar position. Since it is in our embodiment that we most seem to be affected by the other, Descartes had to take care to divorce his ideal moral agent from her own body as well. Thus when we read "The Passions of the Soul," we find Descartes proposing that the ideal observer is "inside" the body, "seated" in the brain, where rationality dwells.[6] We have a sense from Descartes that a person inside us, abstracted from our body, is struggling for control of the body. According to Descartes, a person is virtuous exactly to the extent that his "rationality" can "take control" of the passions—and especially of their physical dimensions. And so "it is by success in these combats [against the passions] that each individual can discover the strength or the weakness of his soul; for those in whom by nature the will can most easily conquer the passions and arrest the movements of the body which accompany them, without doubt possess the strongest souls" (xlviii).

Descartes, then, came to provide us with our image of the *strong* and virtuous person: one who can *control* his passions and the *reactions* of his body to the *stimulus* of the other. Twentieth century scientific authorities now agree that the Cartesian model of the body, especially in the area of passions, is wholly inadequate. But Descartes' model continues to reign in the popular understanding of virtue. One of the most devastating literary critiques on this form of "taking control" is Joseph Heller's *Something Happened*. In the penultimate scene, the protagonist, Bob Slocum, in trying to prevent his injured young son from crying, suffocates him to death. In the last scene, Martha, the office typist, suffers a breakdown, and he handles the situation well, particularly because he had foreseen it and planned what he would do. As the medical team takes Martha away, Slocum observes, "I hear applause when she's gone for the way I handled it. No one was embarrassed. Everyone seems pleased with the way I've taken command."[7] Even in popular songs, we find evidence of Descartes' influence. Maureen McGovern sings a good Cartesian "pop" song whose lyrics are, "Don't cry out loud./Just keep it inside/and learn how to hide/your feelings."

To adopt the prevailing popular Cartesian model, however, would mean that we would be cut off from passions, and from our body, ironically, especially if we are virtuous and strong. But we can't be. A person would not be fully human without a body, and not be fully moral without finding a way to integrate passions into his moral project. So we have to find a way to recover our passions and become more fully human. And the point is, with the Cartesian model, the only way open to us to recover those conquered passions is to *lose control* of ourselves. The popular Pointer Sisters show their instinctual grasp of that realization when they sing, "I'm so excited./And I just can't hide it./I'm about to lose control and I think I like it."[8]

Descartes' "objectivity," then, has not accomplished his intended integration of the agent. We need a better model for integration of the rationality and physicality of the individual moral agent than the "win-lose," "ghost in a machine" model of Descartes, which ends by dividing the agent against himself. And Descartes' model of moral agency must unfortunately fail in its aspirations for social harmony as well. A strong, objective observer of facts must finally resist anything which might move him, and so adversely influence his moral agency. Such an agent would see the other as not gift, but only as intrusion. One dramatic example of this resistance to the other can be found in an observation by Immanuel Kant, who inherited and continued the Enlightenment project. In his *Religion within the Limits of Reason Alone,* he describes the human condition of "being assaulted by evil principles" as occurring through one's own fault. Thus "when he looks around for the causes and circumstances which expose him to this danger and keep him in it, he can easily convince himself that he is subject to these not because of his own gross nature [*rohen Natur*] so far as he is here a separate individual, but because of mankind to whom he is related and bound." He goes on specifically to attack the passions (such as envy, lust for power, and greed) which "besiege his nature, contented within itself, *as soon as he is among men.* And it is not even necessary to assume that these are men sunk in evil to lead him astray; it suffices that they are at hand, that they surround him, and that they are men, for them mutually to corrupt each other's predispositions and make one another evil."[9] We need a better model for social interaction, since such a moral attitude can never achieve the integration and the peace we seek in our moral project.

Once Descartes and the Enlightenment had framed the question, setting rationality against embodiment, soul against body, moral agency against being moved, we can easily imagine the results for the study of passions. There are many good histories which summarize the course of those reflections.[10] In general we can say that Enlightenment and post-Enlightenment thinkers began to conceive of affectivity as at best a second order process, which occurred either as a *reaction* to an external *stimulus,* or perhaps through some activity of the mind. And all of that prompted ethicists toward an increasing conceptual divorce between reason and the passions because the body was so resistant to *control* by the reason,[11] or by the will.[12] The passions, with their bodily changes, were increasingly seen as *disturbing* the rational processes, and interfering with the rationality or the will of the ideal observer.[13] Cartesian dualism—within the self, and between the self and the other—remained.

Two thinkers provided the ground for contemporary scientific studies on the physical dimensions of the passions. I will use some of their insights to turn our attention back to the body, since I want to unite what has been falsely divided in modern discussions of the passions.

In 1872, Charles Darwin claimed that the process of evolution itself habituated certain "serviceable bodily reactions" in the particular species, such that "actions, which were at first voluntary, soon became habitual, and at last hereditary, and may then be performed even in opposition to the will."[14] Thus he recovered the essential notion of *habit* in affectivity, which Descartes had failed to develop. He also gave us a model that allowed us to see the fundamental and simple roots of all affectivity as *approach or avoidance.* Finally, "he gave numerous illustrations of the basic continuity of emotional expressions from lower animals to humans,"[15] the modern study of which is called

"ethology." Researcher Arthur Peacocke stresses the importance of
that last realization for our modern, environmentally-conscious world
view.[16]

In 1884 William James advanced a thesis which marked a turning point in the history of reflection on the passions.[17] The crucial
change was that James, far from regarding the bodily changes of passions as disturbances, made those changes the center of his account of
affectivity. James' thesis was "that the bodily changes follow directly
the PERCEPTION of the exciting fact, and that our feeling of the same
changes as they occur IS the emotion."[18] James so emphasized the bodily components of passion that he would say that it is not that we cry
because we are sad, it is that we are sad because we cry. There were
problems with such a theory, of course. James leaves undiscussed the
nature of the feeling of the bodily change. Certain macroscopic physical changes, like weeping, are characteristic of different passions, such
as joy and sadness. But James raised the possibility that one could distinguish among feelings precisely by their unique set of bodily
changes, which we will call their *bodily signature*. He suggested that
feelings could be changed by altering the patterns of bodily change.[19]
But his lasting contribution was to invite scientific measurement of,
and experimentation in, the bodily components of the passions. It is to
those contemporary scientific studies that we turn now, to provide us
with the strong physical substratum we need for a richer account of
virtues and passions. As we go through the current neurological and
biochemical research on the passions, we will gradually form a model
for understanding the passions that is faithful to all the data. I have
divided that research broadly into three models, and selected for discussion one researcher who best represents each model.

II. Stimulus-Response Models

In 1885 William James and Danish psychologist Carl G. Lange
cooperated on a book in defense of similar ideas on the passions. There
they suggested that specific emotions would be associated with specific internal organs.[20] However, in 1929, Walter Cannon's study seemed
to disprove the James-Lange theory. Cannon stimulated particular
internal organs, and found that that stimulation did not produce the

requisite corresponding emotional states predicted by the James-Lange theory.[21] So Cannon, and many researchers after him, instead began to postulate that particular passions were associated with particular sections of the brain (the thalamic theory). Experiments gradually refined Cannon's theory, and those who hold that the brain is the locus of affectivity are now called centralists. Contemporary centralists have concluded that the *entire* brain is involved in affectivity, since they have found that similar affective states were evoked even when different sections of the brain were stimulated.[22] But there were those who remained with the James-Lange theory, also in a refined form, who are now called peripheralists. Contemporary peripheralists hold that the primary locus of affectivity is away from the brain, in the autonomic nervous system (ANS), or in parts of the body other than the brain, such as the skin, or the cardio-pulmonary system.

The point is that there is truth in both centralist and peripheralist claims, and the one who has done most to unite those two positions is Karl Pribram. In his research[23] he has discovered important alterations in the electrical rhythms of the brain in response to stimuli. But he has also discovered changes in the body in response to the same stimulus, and so he has tried to bring those two dimensions of affectivity into a unified theory.

Pribram has experimented with animals to discover the biochemical and neurophysiological characteristics of habit, particularly in approach conditioning. In a series of experiments, he taught hundreds of monkeys to distinguish between striped or circular patterns. "Recordings from electrodes implanted in the visual cortex produce wave forms that vary according to whether the monkey sees stripes or a circle. If the monkey is rewarded with a peanut for learning to push left or right panels, depending on whether stripes or circles are seen, then wave forms alter as he educates himself. This learned recognition and his 'intention-to-press' alter the wave forms *before* they register in the visual cortex and before the action is taken."[24]

How can we explain this? Pribram postulates that every organism has a stable baseline which consists of all the functions of the body—heart rate, breathing, hormone levels, etc. The brain, through its chemico-neural activity, maintains an awareness of the dynamic biochemical and neurological stability of the entire body, since "visceral and autonomic events are repetitiously redundant in the history of the organism. They vary recurrently, leading to stable habituations, [and the] habituation to visceral and autonomic activity makes up a large share, although by no means all, of the stable baseline from which the organ's reactions can take off."[25] Then, when a new stimulus is introduced (such as the peanut reward for correct identification of circles or stripes), the entire organism gradually habituates itself to this new reality, until response to that stimulus becomes almost as automatic as breathing.[26]

Pribram's analysis is suggestive for our study, because he is speaking of the biochemical foundation of *habit,* which will figure so prominently in our subsequent discussions of the habit of virtue. At the very least, we now find it impossible to describe the process of being moved in the old way: that an external event is physically perceived, sent to the brain, evaluated, then acted on. Pribram's monkeys were registering intent-to-push *before* the signals reached the processing center (visual cortex) of the brain. It appears, rather, that habituation provides a kind of dossier which is *available to the whole organism,* not just the brain. In habituation, the higher functions of discrimination and intention become features not just of the brain, but *of the body as well.* Put simply, the appropriate interaction has become second nature to the monkeys. Athletes are also familiar with this phenomenon, which they colloquially call "muscle memory."

Central to the formation and maintenance of that unifying habit was the passion of delight—being drawn toward, and repeatedly receiving, that pleasurable peanut. This is important, because it begins to indicate that the body-mind unification of the agent is achieved by being drawn toward an other. Further, the integration is such that certain physical postures and activities and interactions with the environment can begin to structure the mind, and, if habituated through repetition, can dispose the individual organism to "see" new interactions with certain specific features of its environment. An Al-Anon saying reflects that understanding well: Move a muscle, change a thought.[27]

Thus for Pribram, and for most of his contemporaries,[28] affectivity—in this case the desire for the peanut—is characteristic of the *entire organism,* unifying the brain and the peripheral activities. We will call this feature the *organic nature* of affectivity. Affectivity can be habituated by consistent physical demeanors and interactions with the environment. That habituation can be toward or away from the other. (In the latter case, it is called "avoidance conditioning."[29]) In habituation we discover a profound, systemic unity between the higher, cognitive functions of the brain and the perceptions and movements of the body, a unity far removed from Cartesian duality.

There are some deficiencies in Pribram's analysis. Although we have begun to use the word "interaction" in speaking about the relationship between the organism and its environment (which we have broadly called, the "other"), we cannot properly use that grammar to discuss Pribram's model. Pribram sees the affective state not as interactive between the self and other, but primarily as a *closed system* within the individual human organism. That is why, in speaking of the interaction between the self and other, he must accept a stimulus-response, or action-reaction model of affective enactment. He seems unable to view its relationship with the environment in any other way other than as "disturbance" (19) or "interruption" (1984, p. 23), revealing, perhaps, some hidden Cartesian presuppositions in his work.[30] With such a model, it would be difficult for him to explain how to go from passion—a "stop mechanism" (26)—to action. Other researchers have a more sophisticated understanding of affective states and of the organism's relation to its environment.

III. Stimulus-Appraisal-Response Models

Paul Ekman has focused his research on affectivity primarily on facial expressions.[31] His studies are very instructive, principally because they take into account the *meaning* that facial expressions have in affective interaction. He has found, first, that specific passions have specific corresponding facial expressions. He then demonstrated that certain facial expressions were transculturally recognized—even by "visually isolated" dwellers in New Guinea—as expressing certain basic passions, "such as happiness, surprise, fear, anger, disgust, and sadness."[32]

In 1984, Ekman expanded his research to demonstrate that not only the face, but the entire body, has a specific signature for each passion. He did this by asking subjects to mimic specific muscular facial movements particular to certain passions. When they assumed those facial expressions, "heart rate increases of up to 25 beats per minute for anger and 22 beats per minute for fear were observed" (326).[33] The claim that each passion had a specific bodily signature seemed at first to be refuted by Cannon's (1929) research. But scientists now realize that Cannon's research on the viscera was too restricted. They now measure a much broader range of biochemical and neurophysiological factors. Frijda[34] lists those as heart rate,[35] respiration, skin conductance levels[36] and sweating, gastrointestinal and urinary activity, secretory functions, pupillary response, hormonal changes,[37] and electrocortical changes. If we take all those factors into account, then it becomes clear that each individual passion does have its own specific bodily signature.

For example, Frijda notes that gastric activity increases when smelling, seeing, or thinking of food—but also when angry, resentful, or impatient (136). This perhaps explains why many people tend to eat—or develop ulcers—when they are angry. Skin conductance levels decrease markedly among some depressed patients (135). Perhaps this accounts for the lassitude and resistance to activity so typical of depression. The hormone epinephrine causes increase in heart rate and heart stroke volume, constriction of peripheral blood vessels, along with increased respiration rate. And the amount of epinephrine also increases in conditions of "uncertainty and ... not knowing what to do about the situation" (147). Anger has been shown to have an increased diastolic blood pressure in comparison to fear. And "fear, when compared to anger, showed greater average SC [skin conductance level], more muscle tension peaks, higher HR [heart rate], and faster respiration" (163).[38]

Each passion, then, will have its own specific signature. Recently, I had a personal reminder of the truthfulness of those bodily signatures. I was getting an EKG with my yearly checkup, lying on the table with the monitor attached to my chest when the doctor came in. I greeted him with aplomb and even with a certain amount of cheeriness. At the end of the evaluation (keep exercising, come back for another EKG in five years), he casually mentioned, "Your heart rate went up to 99 when I entered the room." I learned again that, no matter how much I might try to mask certain passions like fear and apprehension (perhaps even from myself), in reality I am still being affected; my body can't be fooled.

Our study of the body so far has revealed that in interaction with the other, the body is moved, that is, actually, physically changed, sometimes briefly (called "phasically"), and sometimes more lastingly (called "tonically"), sometimes microscopically (heart rate, for example, or skin conductance level) and sometimes macroscopically (facial expressions), in approach or avoidance with respect to the other. And tonic (prolonged) interaction can *physically reconfigure the body.*[39] That is, after prolonged interaction, we become physically disposed toward continuance of that interaction, because that interaction has, for better or for worse, reconfigured our bodies. We might use the analogy of iron filings on a paper, with a magnet underneath. Eventually the filings on the paper are configured to the magnetic field of the magnet. In the same way, prolonged interaction with a specific other gives a kind of integrating order to the self.

If we reflect, we will find we are familiar with the effects of such affective configuration through interaction. We all see with others, and have experienced for ourselves, times in which we should moderate or terminate a particular relationship. A friend of mine reminded me of this typical human struggle recently when he said, "All the way back to the city I was talking to myself, convincing myself that going out with her was just not good for me; I just shouldn't do it anymore. But then as soon as I saw her again, all that stuff just went out the window."

The fact is that through his previous habitual interaction with his friend, his body had been configured by and to that interaction: neuron paths had been formed, hormonal balances had been achieved, consistent electrocortical activities had been established. He had, in short, become accustomed to her. And "all that [rational] stuff" just couldn't change things so quickly. We become, then, increasingly disposed toward particular interactions, even ones that are not good for us. A clear statement of that good is, of course, the subject of this work, and will be considered in greater detail later. For now, though, we should note that those biochemical and neurophysiological configurations occur whether we are in tonic interaction with a substance, *or a non-substance,* like television, or a person, or even particular patterns of behavior or thought.[40] Understanding all that then, we must give our embodied self new and healthier interactions, and *time* to allow those new interactions to reconfigure us corporeally, if we ever want our passions to change.

So far, we have been concentrating on the bodily activity of the self in passion. But Ekman has further observed that the same basic

universal facial expressions elicited a congruent affective response
from onlookers (1980, 95). That is, happy expressions elicited happy
responses, sad expressions sad responses, and so on. He began to call
those basic facial expressions "elicitors," because they could elicit sadness, or joy, or happiness from others.[41] Ekman describes that
dynamism with a "stimulus-*appraisal*-response" model. This is an
important addition to our understanding of the embodied passions,
because Ekman is demonstrating what we commonly know: the interaction with the other is characterized by *meaning*, which, according to
Ekman and others, must be appraised by the receiving organism before
it can respond. The jump in my heart rate in the EKG room was not
caused only by the physical entry of the doctor into the examining
room. It was caused by the *meaning* of that entry for me. To recall the
story with which this book began, I could tell that Fabian had re-estab-
lished contact (approach) with his younger brother, and that he had
experienced a change of the *meaning* of the interaction, because of the
change of expression on his face.

But exactly in the crucial area of appraisal of meaning, Ekman's
model breaks down over the problem of *time*. With Pribram and others,
he has discovered the near instantaneity of congruent affective
response. So he is compelled to speak of facial elicitors which "can
bring forth emotional reactions near immediately," by an "automatic
appraisal."[42] The problem is that there simply isn't *time* for appraisal as
we commonly understand it. Pointedly, Douglas Hofstadter asks,
"What in the world is going on to enable you to convert from
100,000,000 retinal dots into one single word 'mother' in one tenth of
a second?"[43]

Ekman's need for a separate step of appraisal arises from his
inability to break away from adopting a mind-body dualism, so that if
there is meaning, then it must be evaluated by a rational observer within the body, which then must send commands for what the body must
do. But to introduce a separate act of appraisal creates too many difficulties. First, as we have seen, we cannot account for the nearly instant
affective response to meaning. But also, once we break the organic
unity of affectivity and postulate the need for an isolated act of
appraisal, we find too many other cognitive steps in affectivity which
we must then also account for.[44]

On the other hand, if we were truly to admit the integration of the organic nature of affectivity drawn from our study so far, if we were truly to accept that knowledge is available to the entire organism, and not just the brain, we would have to conclude that in some way, *the body itself shares in rationality*—that the body "knows." Pribram's monkey experiments argue for that conclusion, as do other experiments which report the phenomenon of instant appraisal.[45]

What I am proposing is that the appraisal or evaluation does indeed take place, but not as a separate step, nor by an isolated internal evaluator. Rather, meaning is a feature of the entire interaction between organisms, and *evaluation is a characteristic of the entire embodied organism*. This model, of evaluation as embodied, accounts for the evidence (both scientific and common experience), avoids the pitfalls of postulating an isolated step of appraisal, and gives us a richer taxonomy of the rationality and physicality of the moral agent.

How is that organic integration achieved? By habitual interactions with the other. We have seen that an habitual interaction with the other changes the organism itself, even in its physicality. Certain habitual interactions reinforce and increase the systemic unity of the organism. Other interactions can destroy that unity, as for example in the case of addictions.[46] So it becomes necessary to feel "the right things, at the right time, to the right extent, for the right reason, toward the right person." And again, it is the project of this book to discover what those "right passions" are. But at this point in our investigation, we have discovered that our passions are our experience of being moved by the other. Thus our need for the right passions for the integration of the *self* translates into a need for the right *other* to be *affected by,* so that we as individuals can become organically whole precisely through interrelationships.

IV. An Interactive Model

In the affective give and take of interrelationships, we have been concentrating on the energy coming toward the agent, focusing on being affected, since our study is of the passions. But to complete our scientific model of the passions, we must include scientific reflections on the other in the interaction between organisms, especially since we have discovered that the integration and organic unity of the self requires interactions with the other. That full model of affectivity, including (1) the organic unity of the moral agent, (2) interactions with the other, and (3) the interplay between organic unity and interactions with the other, we will call the *interactive model*.

The first step toward an interactive model comes from Scherer, who defines emotion "broadly speaking as the interface between an organism and its environment, mediating between constantly changing situations and events and the individual's behavioral responses."[47] The idea that passions are features of an interface between the organism and the other is very attractive. But Scherer still partially holds to the stimulus-response model, as revealed by his use of the word "response" as characteristic of that interface. He also shares some of the difficulties of the stimulus-appraisal-response model when he goes on to describe the interface as an evaluation of the relevance of environmental stimuli, preparation of actions, and then communication of reactions to social surroundings (296). By this the self would seek both to "monitor *and modulate*" interactions with the other. In the end, however, Scherer himself would describe his model of the passions more as an "interorganismic *signal* system," than as a true interactive model (296, emphasis added).

The common form of understanding how the human organism modulates his interaction with the environment is by exercising control over the environment—acting upon it so as to change it. But because we are considering the *passions,* we need to explore the ways in which the individual can modulate the interaction by *being changed himself,* or, better, by allowing himself to be changed by the action of an other upon him. And because the affective state is specifically attentive to meaning, I submit that the way to modulate affective interaction is to experience a change in the *meaning* of what is affecting us. Recall again the story of Fabian and his little brother. Once Fabian acquired a new meaning for the actions of his little brother, his relationship to him was changed, deepened; his passions and his emotions changed.

Again, such notions remove us far from the idea of Descartes' objective reality which can be observed by anybody. In the realm of passions, where meaning plays such an important role, the significance of the other is crucial. When Fabian raised his hand to congratulate his little brother, it had another meaning for the young boy, and he was physically moved away by that meaning. Contemporary research increasingly concurs that "beliefs, expectations and motives or commitments influence attention and appraisal at the very outset of any encounter."[48] On the other hand, something with no meaning for the one affected cannot affect it, since the one affected has to have a prior aptitude for something or someone before it can interact with it at all. Put simply, if something has no meaning for us, it literally does not occur to us.

I am not denying the otherness of the other here, because there cannot be interaction except between two. Nor is it possible in the model we are developing to conceive of an organism in passion except with respect to a distinct other. But to be entirely consistent with the interactive model, we would have to conclude that each other has of itself a wide range of possible significances, which wait, as it were, for proper interaction to be fully enacted. Thus the moral agent, at the same time as she is being affected by the other, is, within the same field of interaction, modulating the other as well, by *taking the other in a certain way*—with a certain meaning. Interaction with the right agent, then, in the right way, at the right time, would fulfill the nature of the other in the right way as well. In other words, the meaning of an interaction is determined interactively. Hofstadter advances the same idea when he writes, "This way that any perceived situation has of seeming to be surrounded by a cluster, a halo, of alternative versions of itself, of variations suggested by slipping any of a vast number of features that characterize the situation, seems to me to be at the dead center of thinking."[49] This notion is not at all foreign to those of us who have responsibility for young people, since we know that if we consistently take a young person to be a particular kind of person, he or she will inevitably become that particular kind of person. More frequently than we imagine, it is true of adults with whom we interact as well.

Each affected individual can be attuned to different meanings of the other, such that she is moved to approach or avoidance. That feature of agency we will call *disposition*.[50] The organism develops those dispositions precisely through interaction. And the most apt, or congruent interaction for the one affected is interaction with its own kind or species. It seems logical, then, to look for the origin of those individual dispositions in the first interactions of an individual, in infant-caregiver relationships. Many researchers have examined those primary relationships. Their studies are important for us here because those primary interrelationships establish dispositions which will continue to characterize the individual's interaction with the other throughout its history. In fact, if there is any one feature which we might say constitutes the nature of living organisms, it is the immutable need to interact, especially with similar organisms. Recall that interaction can be characterized by approach or avoidance. But it seems true that without prolonged (tonic) bonding (approach) with similar organisms, the life of the organism disintegrates. Several experiments with young animals confirm this.

When J.P. Scott[51] separated three-week-old puppies from their mothers, he found that the puppies yelped at a constant 100 yelps a minute. He used that objective numerical factor to measure the effectiveness of various attempts to calm the puppy. The yelping remained constant if he gave it food or a new object; it decreased slightly if he gave it a soft object or introduced an unfamiliar puppy; it decreased markedly when a familiar puppy was introduced; and showed the most decrease when the experimenter gentled the puppy (46-48). We notice several important aspects of this experiment which are pertinent for our own study. The first is that interaction seems to require warm *physical* touching: the soft object calmed better, and the gentling by the experimenter calmed best in the absence of the mother. The second is that there seems to be a need for *meaning* in successful interaction: the familiar puppy calmed better than the strange puppy, though there could be little physical difference between the two. The third is that the puppy seemed to require that physical, significant interaction more than food itself, since introducing food to the puppy didn't calm its separation distress at all.

Thus research has revealed that living organisms have a nature which requires physical, bonding interaction with a living other, usually a similar organism, who is significant to that organism. Without such interaction, the organism disintegrates, as did the monkeys in the well-known Harlow and Harlow experiments.[52] But McNaughton reports a more complex experiment which underscores the profoundly interactive nature of those primary relationships. Fear and anxiety were artificially induced in certain mother rats while they were pregnant. Predictably, the fear and anxiety were passed along to their young when they were born. When these "fearful" mother rats were given rat pups from a "normal" mother, those rat pups gradually began to interact with fear and anxiety. But most interesting is that when the newly-born rat pups of the "fearful" mother were immediately taken and given to a "normal" mother, the normal mother began after a time to interact with fear and anxiety.[53]

Given the background of our study so far, we can explain the results of McNaughton's experiment. The individual organism has been configured to fear as an organic whole. That organic configuration can take place through interaction, even with no cognitive participation on the part of the organism, since the rat pups were conditioned in the womb. The organism then goes on to *take* an other in the same fearful way (that is, with a certain meaning), with the result that fear (in this case) informs and characterizes all its subsequent interactions with the other. *Passions*, then, *are learned* from early embodied interactions between infants and caregivers. The organism's dossier is first assembled in those interactions. And those learned, embodied passions then continue to *dispose* the organism to take its subsequent interactions with the other in a certain way. That taking of the other in a certain way, with a certain meaning, under a certain description, modulates the other (in the last case, the rat pups modulating the "normal" mother to become fearful) from within the interaction.

Those studies with other living organisms have indicated that infant-caregiver relationships are crucial for learning passions and developing the dossier of meanings and dispositions for the organism. As we might expect, researchers have discovered similar needs for the human organism. In fact, many contemporary studies indicate that human affectivity is best understood as interactive among human beings.[54] L. Alan Sroufe, for example, states that "[a]ttachment (the affective bond between infant and caregiver) is a key construct in this organizational view of infant emotional development, because it lies at the intersection of affect and cognition."[55] He points out that it is exactly in the field of that interaction that we find integration between the rational and physical dimensions of the child.

For the remainder of this section, we shall focus on human infant-caregiver relationships, using the studies of Colwyn Trevarthen. Trevarthen's work is important because it gives us insights into the truly interactive nature of affectivity among humans. We can find in those primary human interactions the genesis of the dossier of meanings and dispositions which will be characteristic of the individual agent throughout her history. Let us now briefly discuss his findings.

Simply put, Trevarthen's study has led him to conclude that human affectivity is *constitutively interrelational*. That is, "emotions are inseparable from contacts or relationships between persons. Where there is an emotion expressed or felt, this will relate to a mental representation of another person who may be affected by that emotion. Emotions are not part of the mental processes of isolated subjects as such."[56] Far from being bounded entirely within the organism, then, passions are interrelational phenomena.

Trevarthen conducted experiments with infants and caregivers which confirm the interrelational nature of embodied passion. He had observed that "after six weeks normal infants readily engage in precise interaction with their mothers by means of facial vocal and gestural expression," to the point where those interactions "produce coincident or reciprocal displays" between caregiver and child (131), establishing, in other words, a completely interactive relationship. Notice Trevarthen's acknowledgment of the simultaneity characteristic of affective interaction. He avoids Cartesian stimulus-response grammar, and instead reports on passions that are "coincident and reciprocal." Since that interaction is so thoroughgoing, Trevarthen asserts that infants feel adult emotions, and vice versa (150). He noted that "this sharing by means of coordinated orientations to surroundings and to each other allows the growth of *meanings*," as we would expect (132, emphasis added).

Trevarthen filmed a "happy" interaction between mother and baby, using three cameras and three positions, one of the mother and baby happily together, one only of the baby in that happy interaction, one only of the mother in that same happy interaction. Later on, he showed the video of the face on the happily interacting mother to the infant. But the infant showed marked signs of distress in viewing the video. Even more interestingly, when he showed the video of the face of the happily interacting infant to its mother, *she* showed distress, asking what might be wrong with her child. And so he concludes "that, for both mother and baby, the form and responsiveness of expressive behavior determines its affective message. Emotions were *in the interactive relationship* of expressive behaviors" (145, emphasis added). That is, even though the facial expressions were objectively happy, they were anomalous, and even disturbing, to the original interactors themselves because they were on video, and not in living interrelationships. We see, too, how this experiment disproves the theory that affective expressions are "signals" to others (which must be "appraised" in a separate step, then "responded to"). If affective expressions were merely signals, the video would have been enough to elicit the "happy" response from the mother and infant.

Thus to have the right meaning, passions and their attendant bodily changes have to be *lodged in an actual interpersonal relationship.* Affectivity is constitutively interactive. For clarity, we can distinguish between two *poles* of the interaction. But the affectivity is *in the interaction* of those two poles, an interaction which, as we have seen, affects each organism.

Let us briefly sum up our discoveries. We have discovered that every interaction has a meaning that is lodged in the interaction. We have concluded that each meaningful interaction moves us organically (in our rationality and physicality), reconfiguring us either phasically if the interaction is brief, or tonically if it is prolonged. After tonic interactions, especially with primary caregivers, we have become *disposed* toward certain kinds of interactions with an other. That is, even when we are physically removed from such interactions, we are still attuned to, looking for, those same kinds of familiar interactions with an other. That is why, perhaps, we find that so many battered spouses grew up in abusive families. The patterns learned there have become familiar, have become embodied, and so are repeated in the marriage.

As we have said, if there is anything which is natural for the organism, it is its openness to interaction; it is natural for us to be in interaction. It is true that as we grow, we develop ego boundaries that are healthy to keep. But as we have seen, we literally learn how to feel from our primary interactions, and from them we acquire the dispositions which remain through our life (unless intentionally changed). In the same way, the essential interactive quality of affectivity remains as well. In fact, most recent studies reveal that we begin to "pick up" emotions from people within about a tenth of a second of coming into association with them. Our body chemistry and neurology begin to reconfigure according to the other's moods.[57]

Thus, to achieve an interaction that supports and enhances the organic unity of both poles of the interaction is "rare, praiseworthy and

noble," to quote Aristotle. That is why to achieve successful interaction in later life is a *virtue*, and that is why, in turn, that the passions
are the material of virtue. Much current research, and our own analysis
of the deficiencies of other models, support Trevarthen's interactive
model for affectivity. It is that interactive model that we will employ in
this book. And again, in the give and take of affective interaction, we
will continue to focus on the dimension of "being moved"; we will
continue to concentrate on the passions.

It would be well to end this chapter by remembering the story
with which I began this book, the story of Fabian reaching out to his
"little brother" at the orphanage. There was a certain power or energy
between them. At first the direction of the interaction was negative,
characterized by avoidance. Fabian's little brother avoided his out-
stretched hand; in turn Fabian himself withdrew. Notice how their bodies were inevitably involved in this interchange. But when Fabian
experienced a change of meaning, his passions changed. I know now
that he changed neurophysiologically and biochemically at that point.
Then, I could see the change on his face. I could see it in his return to
the soccer field. His passions now empowered him to approach, to
bond with the young boy. The young boy's cowering away no longer
threatened Fabian; it "moved him" to compassion, moved him toward
his little brother. And what was wonderful for me was that I was part
of the community which helped Fabian to sustain that meaning in the
subsequent months, and so to sustain what became a relationship
which changed us all. That physical touch of the other, which we are
by nature disposed toward, which we desire more than food, became
possible for Fabian and his little brother. And as for me, I began to
learn a little more about hope, which Aquinas says is a passion caused
by love.

We have not yet told Fabian's story well enough. We still need
to bring our discussion to philosophers and theologians to gain a richer
understanding of affectivity, and of the passions. We will approach
them now, bringing with us the interactive model from the research of
this chapter.

2.

PHILOSOPHICAL AND THEOLOGICAL APPROACHES TO THE PASSIONS

As persons of character we do not confront situations as mud puddles into which we have to step; rather the kind of "situations" we confront and how we understand them are a function of the kind of people we are.
— Stanley Hauerwas, *A Community of Character*

Philosophical and theological literature on the passions is quite extensive. In this chapter we will review several contemporary accounts of the morality of the passions. By reviewing those few specifically, we hope to discover some weaknesses generally shared by modern accounts of the passions. At the same time, we hope to present a more thorough understanding of the interactive model we have developed from our scientific studies in the first chapter.

In general, contemporary ethicists seek to tell us how we can be responsible moral persons, that is, moral agents. William C. Spohn suggests that "recent discussion on passions and principles among philosophers and psychologists illumines the interplay of reason and affectivity in moral experience."[1] But our research reveals that most contemporary ethicists are still subtly affected by a Cartesian dualism, and by an Enlightenment understanding of the "rational" agent as an unaffected observer who objectively examines facts and acts on them. Inattention to those deep presuppositions usually means that ethicists fail in their understanding of the organic unity of the person (especially in her embodiment), and in their understanding of the interactions between the self and the other. With such an understanding of moral agency, it is impossible to give an adequate moral account of the *passions* since, as we have seen, the Enlightenment tradition is to consider our being affected as somehow opposed to our rationality. In fact, as we will see in this chapter, to account for the passions, we need to break free of that constricting Enlightenment notion of rationality, and propose a much richer understanding of the nature of moral agency. Let us turn to that discussion now.

I. Stimulus-Response Models

In some cases, the reliance on the Cartesian model is explicit, as with J.R.S. Wilson,[2] or W.D. Hart.[3] Wilson, for example, states that emotion and its object are "two different 'items' in the world," and that the relationship between those two items is such that the "mental causes the physical" (30), that the mind acts directly upon a physical body in a cause–effect relationship. These presuppositions suffer from the same inadequacies as do Descartes'. The principal difficulty is that once we have dichotomized mental and physical, making them totally separate states, we have no way of explaining how the mental would ever act on the physical, or vice versa. A modern way to say this would be: How can something without mass affect something with mass, and vice versa? Descartes had to postulate a "little gland" in the brain as a sort of translation point between those two states—mental and physical—within the human person. But he could not escape the problem by miniaturizing it, since no matter how much he tried to reduce the gap between spirit and matter, he could finally give no account of how the incorporeality of spirit could move the corporeality of matter. This disregard for embodiment in favor of an isolated mental state is typical of those who consciously or unconsciously adopt a Cartesian model.[4] Hart, for example, rather strangely seeks to provide the reader with "a recipe for the visual experience you would have of yourself *without eyes or a brain*."[5] Let us look further at this model of the mental causing the physical, and discover some of its chronic difficulties.

Cartesian-based ethicists are aware that we can be moved by the other, but that causes three major problems. First, if they are to be truly moral in this model, they must have a world where only the mental (or rational) moves the physical. Thus they would have difficulty explaining why a non-rational thing, like a flower for example, can make us happy. Second, they would have even further difficulty explaining why and how the self would move to smell the flower, or present it to someone else. Third, and most importantly for this study, Cartesian-based philosophers cannot explain how we come to the right evaluation of the other, so that our actions toward the other can be right.

Cartesian-based philosophers usually respond to the first problem by saying that an object causes emotion not of itself, but by the mental freight we impart to it from earlier and/or similar encounters. Thus Wilson writes that the "thought-about object relates to emotion only if the object played a certain part in the genesis of a dossier on which thought draws."[6] On that model, even though it may appear that we are being moved by the other, we are in actuality being moved by our own mind. But this strategy must fail. Primarily, we must ask how the mind acquired the previous dossier from which it invests the present object with value. For example, when a new-born infant is in interaction with its caregiver, what "previous dossier" can it draw upon? In technical analytical language, the model falls to infinite regress. The passions—the acquisition of the dossier—had to start somewhere. But because Cartesian-based philosophers are presuppositionally turned against the body as inferior to the rational, they can have no ground in basic bodily needs (like touch, for example, or food) from which to begin the moral trajectory of the passions. Soon we will also see how such a model must even resist the reality of the other.

An alternate solution to the first problem of "being moved" is sometimes offered by dividing the self into two parts, as Descartes himself did. Thus Dent, for example, states that the "sense-pleasure" that we take in the other is not "good-dependent" (45), whereas passions come from the mental activity of investing value in the other (62). Thus "[t]he having of passions is dependent upon one's making valuations, whereas having sense-desires is not" (64).[7] There are difficulties with this alternative vision of the divided self as well. It becomes impossible to conceive of interacting with the good as pleasurable—that we might actually enjoy doing the right thing and feeling the right way, because of the pleasurable attractiveness of the good in the other. Recall that Aristotle, in the *Nicomachean Ethics*, tells us that one way to look at the moral project is to speak of having pleasure and pain at the right things. In short, we *should* take pleasure exactly in being moved by, and doing, the good. That is the sign of a virtuous person. And if we are just, let us say, we should be in pain if we perform an unjust act, precisely in that something of us has *broken*; we have *broken the habit* of being just. An advantage of the interactive model is that we can state that the value of the other moves the self *organically*, that a passion is an *embodied* experience of the value of the other in terms of meaning. Thus we *can* account for taking pleasure—with all its "messy" physicality—in a just act. We can, in the words of the Sermon, quite literally *"hunger and thirst* for justice"— and be satisfied.[8]

The second major problem for Cartesian-based philosophers is to account for how the self gets from being moved to acting, from being moved by a flower to smelling or presenting it. Again we face the difficulty of how a non-corporeal mental state can cause action in a physical body. But even more, Cartesian-based philosophers can never reconcile themselves to the fact that the other moves us somehow. They are presuppositionally committed to calling these movements "disturbances" of the rational, sheerly mental agent. Dent, for example, tells us that we cannot be "in thrall" to feelings and desires, since then we would be "acted upon and not agents...subjects and not masters" (121). He cautions us not to let our passions "possess us, take us over" (134), but to modify them by a "practical rational judgement...which takes the form of bringing an 'external' check upon the arousal and expression of sense-desire" (142).[9] With respect to passions, Cartesian-based philosophers see the moral project as a struggle for *control* of the passions by the reason. It is a struggle for control of the other as well, since we do not want to be "in thrall" or "possessed." We want to be *agents,* we are told, and not to be acted upon; we do not want to be moved. In the end, the two oppositions (between the self and the other, and between the self and its embodied reality—entail each other, since the other is intruding upon the rational, mental self) *and is intruding by virtue of the self's own embodiment.*

When we consider the organic unity of the interactive model, however, and its attention to the body, we recall that the very act of perception is characterized by a biochemical or neurophysiological movement toward or away from the other, that passions are the embodied perception-appraisal of the other by the self. In the interactive model, then, the ground, the locus, for the interchange of passion and action is in the body itself. That is, the body is already in act by the very fact of perception. But this brings us to our last problem: How can we know if those incipient movements of approach or avoidance are right? To use our example again, how can we know if it is right to smell or to run away from a flower, to present it to someone or to stamp on it?

Cartesian-based philosophers do recognize that we can have wrong passions. Because passions are caused by mental investments of the self in the other, however, their system can offer no plausible way that the self can even detect, let alone change, its wrong passions. If the change is effected by another, then that is intrusion. If the self is aware of a commotion between the mind and the passions, how can the self distinguish between the commotion that is the normal moral struggle for control, and the commotion that occurs when the other is a good, and the mind resists it because of a previous dossier?

On the other hand, consider the interactive account of how wrong passions occur, and how they can be corrected. Recall the seemingly deterministic interaction of the frightened rat pups with the normal mother; gradually the normal mother began acting frightened as well. With this in mind, notice the meaning Fabian's little brother first gave to Fabian's raised hand. To him it meant physical abuse, though its true meaning was congratulation and support. The little boy was feeling the wrong way, at the wrong time, toward the wrong person. Nonetheless, because of the power of interaction, and our constant need for it, his other (Fabian) was partially determined by the little boy's dispositions, so that Fabian withdrew in confusion, as had the little boy himself. But in the interactive model, the other has its own distinct reality (otherwise there can be no interaction). Its affective meaning is not entirely determined by the dossier of the one with which it is in interaction. Fabian was able, through other, proper interactions, to insist upon his otherness to the dossier of abuse, and so regain and sustain his own meaning (of congratulation and support) in the interaction with his little brother. Thus Fabian and his community eventually overcame the little boy's fear, and allowed right passions in interaction. Later we will see that Aquinas, and our shared passion for justice, insist that the sign of the Spirit is exactly this freedom from another's compulsion.

That last point brings us to our final observation in bringing the interactive model into discussion with modern Cartesian thought on the passions. Since we are considering the interactive model, we must state that the self not only imparts value to the other, it also receives value from the other in the mutual dynamic of interaction. The other is not value-neutral; it has a value in and of itself. Then we can understand passions as *an embodied experience of the value of the other.*

Since the other has a value in itself, and its value cannot be wholly determined by the other, then the interactive model would require that we must take care that the meaning that we have for the other is *congruent,* or *fitting,* to its own intrinsic value. In this way, our moral task would be to come to appreciate the significance of the other, to "take" the other in the right way. Consider, for example, the person who is obsessed with gaining an impregnable financial security. For her, the meaning of the other (in this case, money) is out of proportion with, incongruous to, its own intrinsic value. She must learn to take it in the right way, and for that, community support would be indispensable. Later in this chapter we will submit that the interactive model offers a powerful insight on how to accomplish this moral task. But for now, let us examine some philosophic positions which consider the importance of *appraisal* in their accounts of the morality of the passions.

II. Stimulus-Appraisal-Response Models

In this section, we will encounter two schools of thought on affectivity which emphasize the importance of *appraisal* in their discussions of the passions: Motivationists and Cognitivists. Broadly speaking, Motivationists hold that emotions such as love or desire or greed are motives for our actions, and, since we are responsible for our actions, our emotional motivations deserve consideration in any account of moral agency. Cognitivists stress the cognitive dimension of passions, again because it seems easier for them to give an account of moral agency if they underscore those "mental" features of affectivity (appraisals, beliefs, judgments, etc.) which seem to be more voluntary. Both schools, then, attempt to tell us how we can be morally responsible for our passions, but still under the rubrics of some form of *action* theory. Currently, ethicists have begun to refer especially to Cognitivists as Constructivists.

The model of passion employed by both schools seems to be that something is perceived, appraised, then acted upon. Thus Magda Arnold's well-known definition of emotion is, "the felt tendency toward anything intuitively appraised as good (beneficial) or away from anything intuitively appraised as bad (harmful). This attraction or aversion is accompanied by a pattern of physiological changes organized toward approach or withdrawal."[10] We can see, however, an immediate difficulty for those who employ this model, evidenced in Rorty's own grammar. The problem is: How can we get from appraising a thing, to acting upon our appraisal? Rorty (and with her, both schools of thought) always struggles with this difficulty. In 1960, she wrote that the perception "is accompanied by" bodily changes. In 1970, she wrote that "if nothing interferes, the felt tendency will *lead to* action."[11] In 1984, she wrote that "[w]hen the reward is perceived and appraised, an action impulse is initiated that eventually *leads to action.*"[12] For all her attention to the science of the body in her studies, Arnold has not "closed the gap" between the mental activity of appraisal, and the physical activity of action. Her presentations, and those of the Motivationists and Cognitivists, present the bodily components of the passions always as a kind of second order process, ancillary to the first order mental process of appraisal. And whereas their stress on appraisal attends to the importance of meaning for an affective interaction, their portrayal of appraisal as a sheerly mental phenomenon fails to account adequately for how physical acts might emerge from such appraisals.[13]

From the perspective of virtue, however, there is a deeper problem with the stimulus-appraisal-response model. The problem is that appraisal is a much more complex feature of interaction than the model can portray. Aristotle draws our attention to this in the *Nicomachean Ethics* when he writes, "But someone might argue as follows: 'All men seek what appears good to them, but they have no control over how things appear to them; the end appears different to different men.' If, we reply, the individual is somehow responsible for his own characteristics, he is similarly *responsible for what appears to him* [to be good]"

(1114a32-1114b3, emphasis added). A fuller understanding of this feature of virtue ethics, illuminated by our interactive model, can help us to understand how we can, in Aristotle's words, be responsible for what appears to us—for our appraisals. And let me illustrate this understanding of moral responsibility with a story.

When I was younger, I studied karate for a few years, going three times a week for practice. One day, two fellow students of theology and I decided to go to a movie. Fran was a former Marine sergeant. John was a bright and articulate student. After we had bought our tickets individually, we regrouped in the lobby. "Did you see that guy on the other side of the ticket booth?" Fran asked me. "Yeah," I replied. "He sure was cruisin' for a bruisin', wasn't he?" "You know," Fran said, "the look on his face...I was just waiting for him to try something," and he put his right fist into his left palm. I started to say, "If he made a move on me, I would've..." but John interrupted us by saying, "What guy?"

The facts are these: Fran and I saw this young man, and were ready even to fight with him. John, a bright and alert person, didn't even perceive him. Why? The key lies in our respective backgrounds. In our history, Fran and I shared a training in violence. It was, significantly, a *physical* training which *disposed* us to "take things in a certain way." Specifically, we were "looking for trouble." And we found it. John, with no such training, didn't even perceive the "belligerent" young man.

Reflecting on such an incident from an interactive model, we can begin to give a fuller account of why we can be morally responsible for "what appears to us," as Aristotle has said. Recall some of our observations, now, from the first chapter: If something has no meaning for us, it literally does not occur to us. John, with little belligerence in his dossier, did not perceive the belligerent man. This is itself morally laudable, as Paul indicates in requiring the Corinthians to be "babes with respect to evil" (1 Cor 14:20). It is an interesting feature of the virtuous person that there are some things which it would literally not occur to him to do, or to feel.[14] But examine the interaction of Fran and me with the young man near the ticket booth. I am not saying, with the Cartesian-based authors, that there was no belligerence in the man at the ticket booth, that Fran and I "invested" that belligerence into him, and then reacted to it. I am saying that there was belligerence there, but that Fran and I were particularly attuned to it, since we had acquired a dossier of violence through previous interactions. The point is that there were many features of the young man near the ticket booth. But of the wide range of his possible significances as an other, Fran and I were attuned to, and so fixed upon, his belligerent aspect. That fixation of ours then characterized our interaction with him and enacted that particular meaning for him. If indeed we had fought the man, that enactment of him as belligerent would have been far more dramatic, visible—and fixed. But I have no doubt that even our facial expressions and posture in interaction with him at that time reinforced that particular aspect of his reality.

Reflecting on such incidents can help us give a better account of how we are morally responsible for our passions, for being affected. It may not yet be possible for us to be "babes with respect to evil" (though I do believe that that is one of the rewards of the virtuous life). But we are still morally responsible for how we take the other. In this case, the constant physical activity and constant association with one particular community was disposing me to certain feature-specific interactions with the other—in this case, with violence. And I believe that I could see my deficiency precisely because of my association with John and others like him in another community. And more profoundly, I had an alternate vision of relationships because of my living in the Company of Jesus. In the end, it meant that I had to leave the karate class, and allow those more peaceful community interactions to configure, to characterize my life. And the advantage to this is not only that we simply withdraw from evil, or that we do not interact with the possible evil in the other. The advantage is that, of the cluster, or halo, of possible meanings of the other, we focus on peace, on justice, on compassion. And, like Fabian in the story, supported by a true community, we foster those features of the other in our interactions, thus improving the other and ourselves as well.

In the interactive model, we have established that meaning is a feature of the entire interaction between organisms, and that evaluation (appraisal) is a characteristic of the entire embodied and historical organism. Thus the body is already in act, at least incipiently, by the very fact that the self is in passion. That is, because passions are embodied perception-appraisals, we are already being moved toward or away from the other. Then our problem is not how to get from the mental to the physical, but how to be moved in the right way, at the right time, for the right reason, etc. It seems to me, however, that philosophers have also failed to give a good account of how we would change passions that are wrong, and how in the first place we would even be able to judge that they were wrong. To demonstrate this, let us turn to Amélie Rorty's story of Ella and Louis.

In *Mind in Action: Essays in the Philosophy of Mind* (1988), Rorty summarizes much of her previous work. She recognizes that current theories of affectivity suffer from an inheritance that had treated emotions sometimes as "noncognitive invasions or disturbances," or sometimes as "sound motivational functions, susceptible to a program of rational reform or corrections." For her part, Rorty attempts a more unified approach,[15] and so presents "analyses of a number of psychological activities—love, jealousy, the fear of death, self-knowledge—to show that they are all cognitive, motivational, and affective."[16]

Rorty describes emotion in terms of intention,[17] and then attempts to describe how people change emotions "that they judge to be inappropriate or irrational" (121). She acknowledges the force of *habit* as well. Rorty understands that simply changing a belief does not always change the emotion, since "[t]he conservation of emotions has its explanation in the conservation of habit, especially of those magnetized dispositions involved in selective attention and focused interpretation" (119). Nevertheless, we can change our emotions by changing our habituations, by underwriting secondary emotions, or by knowing the "causal history" of our emotions (121). The interactive model shares Rorty's concern with the "causal history" of passions. From studying Rorty, we can highlight an important dimension of passions. Because passions have a causal history, we can understand passions as experiences of the past coming into interaction with the present. What is more, establishing that trajectory from past to present invites us to project the possible path of passion into the future, and to consider the value of constancy in passion. And that is exactly what Rorty attempts in the story of Ella and Louis.[18] When discussing Ella's hope for Louis, Rorty writes:

> This is a complex and compounded hope: that Louis's love
> will be formed by his perceiving—his accurately perceiv-
> ing—the gradual changes in her, and in his responses being

appropriately formed by those changes. If Ella and Gloria love Louis, they want the changes they effect in him to be consonant and suitable to him as well as to them, conducing to his flourishing as well as theirs. It is because they want their love to conduce to his flourishing that it is important that they see him accurately and that their interactive responses to him be appropriate (124).

And Rorty ends by describing such a love as "dynamically permeable."

The model certainly sounds attractive. It shares many features with the interactive model that we have been developing, including habit and historicity in passions, interaction between the self and the other as constitutive of passions, and the necessity to take the other in the right way. But we are left with some difficulties which, to her credit, Rorty herself recognizes. Seeking to redress those difficulties with Rorty can help clarify and enrich the interactive model of affectivity.

The first difficulty is that there seem to be competing claims in this model. It can occur that the flourishing of one party in the relationship can take place at the expense of the other. Rorty gives us no way to adjudicate those competing claims. Instead, she proposes what she elsewhere in the volume (323) calls as "system of checks and balances." Thus "[s]tandardly, but not necessarily, rationality, appropriateness, and thriving are interwoven…rationality (as defined by truthfulness supported by validity) is a central guide to appropriateness, and appropriateness a central guide to flourishing" (134). But that is not helpful, since even rationality can degenerate into mere expressions of preference, as MacIntyre characterizes modern liberal thought in Chapter XVII of his *Whose Justice? Which Rationality?* But again, how would we choose those criteria? More importantly, *why* would we choose certain emotions over others? Thus Rorty herself recognizes that she has given us no internal means to prevent Louis and Ella's relationship from "being formed by mere perceptions of the moment, to avoid the *folie à deux* problem" (133).[19]

There is a further difficulty with the choice of "flourishing" as one of the values of a relationship. Without any further constraints, it may even occur that one flourishes exactly in taking advantage of another in a relationship. In an insightful article, Sarah Conly draws our attention to just such a problem in her discussion of Lorenzo the

Magnificent. After pointing out that Lorenzo flourished personally, and had even caused Florence to flourish, Conly reminds us that Lorenzo was a consummately unjust man, using treachery and assassination to secure his position. "Nor," she continues, "is this an isolated example."

> An individual can hone his skills, develop his talents, cultivate his tastes, and be happy without a sense of justice. A society with no concept of justice can succeed, and its citizens can flourish, in a sphere where a sense of justice is not expected of them.... [Thus] the inference from X's flourishing to X's virtuousness is unjustified.... While an individual, to flourish, needs a community of a certain order, it does not look as though his own flourishing requires his supporting the community in the way we would consider just, or courageous, or even kind.[20]

Rorty closes her essay by stating that these questions remain unanswered: "How dynamically permeable should Louis be without endangering his integrity or joining Ella in a case of *folie à deux*? How ramified or regionalized should his responses be? What *does* rationality require? What *would* constitute thriving? How are the thriving of Louis, Ella, Louis-and-Ella to be appropriately weighted when they seem to go in different directions?" (134). Rorty suggests that the only way they can answer these questions is by themselves, within the relationship: "It is only the details of their particular situation that can determine what would be rational, what would be appropriate, what would constitute (whose?) thriving." So in the end, Ella and Louis don't seem to have such an attractive relationship after all. Crucial moral questions seem to be unresolved. Ella and Louis don't even seem to have secured the constancy which Rorty sought for them at the outset.

Our discussion with Rorty benefits us, especially in the insight that passions have a trajectory, from the past into the present, and thus from the present into the future. And since Rorty shares much in common with the interactive model, the self-admitted difficulties in her presentation might help us to clarify what the interactive model must offer to be successful. First, let us attend to the trajectory of passions.

In our discussion with Rorty, we have seen that passions have a historicity, a trajectory through time. But that historicity can be flawed, as was that of Fabian's little brother, and so our passions can be a wrong interaction of the past with the present. Rorty's unsuccessful attempt to project passions into the future shows that passions can be inconstant even when constancy is devoutly desired. But recall our earliest statements, that passions were the matter, the stuff, of virtue. Virtue ethicists stress that virtue gives order to human action. Frequently, though, we understand that order to be a *static* order, something like the arrangement of utensils on a table. I submit that because of the nature of habituation—its repetition through time—one of the tasks of virtue is to impart to passions a dynamic, habitual constancy through time. Thus the unity of a moral agent is an appropriate historical trajectory from past to present to future. A virtuous agent would have her past interacting with her present in the right way, at the right time, etc. Such an agent would be able to envision the future of this interaction, seeing the present not only through the history of the past, but also from the perspective of an appropriate final goal, thus achieving a historical unity of vision, and of passion.

In our discussions with philosophers on the passions, we have continued to develop the interactive model. We have seen that the distinctiveness, the *organic nature* of the self and of the other must be preserved in interaction, while at the same time saying that the nature of each is at least in part determined by interactions. If we combine these two realizations, we would have to state that the interaction cannot wholly define either interactor. Each "pole" in the interaction is partially realized, and partially in potential. Put negatively, the nature of the self or other can be destroyed, but is not infinitely malleable in interaction.

We have also discovered that primary interactions between infants and caregivers form, through habit, the dossier of the self, by which it is disposed to certain feature-specific interactions with others. But the logic of the previous paragraph leads us to state that even those primary interactions are not completely formative of the self. We must state that there is a distinctiveness to every human that precedes even such primary interactions. Aristotle would call that distinctiveness "human nature," and would say about human nature that it is possessed at least of the ability to *receive* those habits through interaction (*NE*, II

1103a:24-25). Modern research in "pan-cultural human emotions" and pan-cultural human expressions supports that notion that there is a certain universal intractability to human nature—in its grief, in its joy, in its pain, in its pleasure, in its very need for interaction—which can only be overlaid by what Ekman called "cultural display rules." In human interactions, when we seek to feel "the right way, at the right time, to the right extent, toward the right person," we must value the requirements of that human nature.

We have also stated that, inasmuch as the self is disposed by previous habituation to take the other in certain ways, the experience of passion is an historical experience, bringing past into interaction with the present. Our analysis of Rorty also showed that the historicity of the passions must also extend toward a future goal, and a morally desirable future goal is the preservation, or constancy, of right passions. Conly's corrective reminds us that such a future goal must regard not only flourishing, but also justice as values to be preserved. But the regarding of the future is an eminently rational activity, to be integrated with our commonly experienced desire that a particular sensate delight might never end. Thus proper passions integrate the self (mind and body), have a proper historicity from past to present to future, and are characterized by an appropriate (just) regard for the value of the other. Such a habit of passion would be virtuous.

But now we must unite the themes of nature and historicity. Our final end is to be fully moral beings, and this goal is attained by an historical progression of right interactions, beginning with a distinctive human nature which must be preserved. Then there must be an historical relationship between the original human nature and the final goal of that human nature. From a recognition of that continuum, two things follow. First, our final goal itself is to be understood relationally, since that is the nature of passions from the first. Second, if our final goal is to become fully moral beings, then we must be born to be moral beings. That is, we are not, from the first, indifferent to being moved by a good or evil other. In some rudimentary way, we experience ourselves as violated by an other that is evil and as enriched or empowered by an other that is good. Put positively, the self is integrated by being drawn through history to a final goal which is fitting to the self who was born. When we have, in our moral project, experienced that our earliest passions for touch and food have become integrated with the richer passions for truth and justice, then we can even more fully appreciate the beatitude of those who hunger and thirst for justice.

I realize here that I have broken from Aristotle in this understanding of human nature as moral. But recall that Aristotle states that bad actions or passions, once they are undertaken and habitualized, cannot be undone. They are, he says, like a stone cast into a pond. The original act is under one's charge, but afterward it is irrecoverable. But our experiences, such as those with Fabian's little brother, and our research, at least from Augustine's *Confessions* onward, tell us differently. We can be redeemed and set right, even from our vices. In claiming an intrinsic moral tendency for human nature, I am preserving two things. I am allowing for the self somehow to *know* that something is wrong with our wrong passions. And by that same ability to know, intrinsic to the self, I am providing the proper other with some fulcrum or foothold, as it were, within the self, such that the reconfiguring of the self—the changing of those vices and adoption of virtues—does not paradoxically require a violation of the self, or a control or erasure of the reality of self by the other. In short, it is natural, and the natural fulfillment of the self (and the other), to be moral.

To satisfy all those requirements for fully moral passions, I propose that we consider a *paradigmatic relationship* for our moral lives, analogous to Aristotle's virtuous expert. Aristotle claims that it is not enough to do or feel the right things. We must do or feel them as a virtuous person does or feels them. He suggests that we can identify such a virtuous person by the fact that the community rewards the virtuous person with praise and respect. But several contemporary theologians have submitted that a relationship with God can provide us with just such a paradigm. In the context of faith and religious experience, then, we will ask theologians to address the question: Can there be a passion for God? And what would such a passion look—or, more properly, *feel*—like?

III. Theological Approaches

One of the most interesting recent books to treat of the passions in prayer is Don Saliers' *The Soul in Paraphrase*. He begins by stating, "Whatever else it may include, the Christian faith is a pattern of deep emotions."[21] What is unique is Saliers' implied distinction between "deep" and "shallow" emotions, and that such deep emotions are a pattern. Saliers chooses the word "pattern" because "[t]here is...a pattern of particular affections which constitute and govern the life of a Christian" (8). He calls those deeper emotions "affections," which are the "basic attunement which lies at the heart of a person's way of being and acting."[22] Those affections are gratitude, holy fear, penitence, joy, suffering, and love of God and neighbor. And they "are what they are by virtue of their objects and the characteristic roles they play in the pattern of our thought and behavior" (7).

In his understanding of patterns of Christian emotions, Saliers comes close to the idea of dispositions which we have developed in the first chapter. Saliers, however, seems not to relate Christian and "human" values, because his religious affections seem different in kind than other passions.[23] Is Christian joy, for example, different than non-Christian joy? Further, we wonder why he chose those affections as characteristic of Christians and not others. For example we frequently see Jesus angry in the scriptures. What role does the particular affection of anger have to play in our Christian thought and behavior?

The last question brings us to a deeper problem in Saliers' treatment. What role does Christ play in Christian prayer and affections? Can we call the prayer he is suggesting interrelational? Apparently not.[24] He states:

> The emotion of the believer is made clear in and through language which attributes certain things to God. Learning this language is like learning both the emotions and the beliefs in their correlation (30).

The verb "attributes" partakes of the sense of "imparting value to" which we have already seen as an inadequate model in human relationships; it would be even more inadequate when used to understand prayer. What is important for Saliers is not that we discover the value of the other, but that we invest meaning in the other. Saliers emphasizes not prayer but the language of prayer. He could, I believe, rescue himself by saying that language is the means by which we train "shallow" emotions to become "deep emotions," or "affections." But he does not, and, again, I believe that is because Saliers seems to regard the "religious affections" as different *in kind* than other affections.

Perhaps Saliers could hold that Christian affections really are different in kind from other affections, if he could argue that Christians claim a unique interrelation with God, characterized therefore by unique passions. But he does not, as revealed by his discussion of the particular affections. Even his words in that discussion give us a sense of removal from the immediacy of interrelation with God. We do not understand God as holy, for example, but "the concept" of God as holy. God does not judge one, one "renders judgement on oneself." We do not suffer in the rupture of our relationship with God, but instead "have the complex object" of "sin before God" (31).

More positively, we see that Saliers is open to the importance of community in the Christian life. He writes that "[t]o mean what one prays" is not the intellectual grasp of theology, but "living out certain emotions regulated by the Christian teachings and the Christian story of God in the world" (64). It is the concern of my work to discover what those passions might be, and how that "regulation" might take place. And it seems to me that one place to look for those answers is in the Christian community.[25]

Having reaffirmed the value of disposition and of the Christian community in Christian passions, let us turn our study to two theologians whose work stresses these themes: James Gustafson and Stanley Hauerwas.

Gustafson's earlier work supports many of our findings on the features necessary for an adequate discussion of the passions in the Christian moral life. In 1975, for example, he frames the important question:

> What consequences might there be for our moral dispositions, affections, and intentions from having an experience of the reality of God, from believing in God? and more particularly, of course, God as known in the Christian faith and tradition?[26]

And Gustafson is consistent in what he means by "dispositions":

> By dispositions I wish to suggest a "manner of life," a "lasting or persisting tendency," a "bearing toward one

another and the world," a "readiness to act in a certain
way."[27]

Further, Gustafson takes on the difficult topic of *character*.[28]
When he profiles a Christian character, he models it after Paul's "gifts
of the Spirit."[29] He tells us that "the experience of the reality of God
evokes, sustains, and renews certain 'sensibilities' or 'senses,'" and
lists them as "a sense of radical dependence, a sense of gratitude, a
sense of repentance, a sense of obligation, a sense of possibility, and a
sense of direction" (1971, p. 92). He does not claim that the list is
exhaustive. But we note that he is careful to "correlate" each "sense"
with "certain dimensions of experiences of God and articulate beliefs
about God." Thus, for example, radical dependence correlates to the
belief in God as Creator, and repentance to the experience of God as
Judge (1971, p. 180).

This correlation of Christian senses to features of the divine is
much more workable, since Gustafson is acknowledging the reality of
the other, as opposed to the "imparting of value," which fails to
account for empowerment by the other. There are a few areas, though,
where I believe my own contribution would be of service.

In the first place, I have throughout been concentrating not so
much on action, as on being affected. Gustafson's work stresses action:
"What ought I to do?" is a constant refrain in *Christ and the Moral
Life*. All his discussions on dispositions and character are in terms of
act, as the above quotes show. When he wants to present us with a
means for considering how we can be morally responsible for our passions, he employs the term "agency," which he describes as "accounting for the capacity to be to some degree self-determining within the
conditions of his nature" (180). Such "self-determination" leaves us
with a problem, for example, explaining Christian obedience, as Jesus
was "obedient, even unto death" (Phil 2:8). Could we not call that
Christian virtue "determination by another," at least in part? Gustafson
is not unaware of Christian "passivity," but he presents it often with
negative overtones, using terms like "limit," or "restraint," and, again,
he implies that the nature of the "image of God" in the human is found
in the human's ability to *act*, even to overcome his "being acted
upon."[30] In fact, in *Christ and the Moral Life*, Gustafson presents an

otherwise very illuminating discussion of Aquinas on virtue, but does not mention the passions at all.[31]

Gustafson's insistence upon the moral agent (and one who is in the image of God) as one who acts, and his resistance to being acted upon, leads us to ask several deeper questions of his work. The first is: What part does *suffering* play in the Christian life? Suffering is certainly too big a topic to be treated here, but at least I want to indicate that the interactive model of passion we have been developing allows for moral significance of suffering in a way that Gustafson's insistence on action does not. Furthermore, as our discussion of passions now enters into the theological realm, we must be attentive to the emphasis in the Christian faith on the suffering of Christ and his insistence that his followers must also suffer. We will address this more extensively in the final chapter.

More than that, the same line of questioning leads us to reflect on the role that Christ plays in the Christian ethics of James Gustafson.[32] When we turn again to examine his Christian "senses," we may agree that they are religious, but inquire to what extent they are distinctively Christian. Cannot a Jewish or Muslim believer have the same "senses," arising from similar "experiences" of God as Creator, Judge, etc.? It would seem so, for they too are "people of the book," the same scripture from which Gustafson finds grounding for his beliefs about God. Gustafson's most extensive work on this question was *Christ and the Moral Life,* though it is more a summary of various other theologians' claims for the significance of Christ for the moral life. Gustafson's own constructive statement about the importance of Christ in the moral life seems to point to Christ as an ideal or as a norm for the Christian. So, for example, he writes that "Christians find in Jesus Christ, both in the faith he proclaimed and in his own life and death and resurrection, a confidence in the goodness, mercy and power of God" (244). But again, can't other figures such as Dorothy Day or Martin Luther King or Gandhi give us confidence in the God of goodness, mercy and power? The difficulty is that, without sufficient attention to the unique way that the Christians are moved by Jesus, Jesus himself ends by being no more than an exemplar—albeit a most important one.[33]

In fact, the two questions, about suffering and the role of Christ, are related to each other. McGill shows this when he argues that the Christian understanding of the divine, suffering Christ had to produce a

new understanding of God as essentially Trinitarian, characterized by
"total and mutual self-giving."[34] Then he points out that the Father
deals with human beings in the same way as he does the Son in the
Trinity.[35] From that, we can see that such a distinctively Christian
notion of God is entirely in keeping with the interactive model of the
passions we have been developing. In our model, Jesus in the flesh is
the point of interaction, of mutual self-giving, between the divine and
the human. We find substance for our faith in the body of Christ, the
church, and together we commune with the Father in his Spirit of
prayer, and in the divine working for justice. With this model I believe
we can be more successful in portraying what Saliers has described:
that "those who pray with Christ are participants in his relationship to
God the Father—the relationship of love and self-giving which is the
Holy Spirit" (76). And all this is made possible because of God's willingness to receive what humans had to give in interrelationship. We
can say that without him, we were unable to live, and without us, he
was unable to die.[36] Even our sins are taken up in this passion, since
"for our sake, God made him who knew no sin to become sin, so that
through him we might become the very holiness of God" (2 Cor 5:21).
By interacting with God in Christ in these ways, the community begins
to understand the passion of God.

The last contemporary theologian-ethicist we will consider is
Stanley Hauerwas. Hauerwas has admitted that he lacks a satisfactory
treatment of passions,[37] but I believe that the interactive model of the
passions can draw together seemingly anomalous elements in his work.

Throughout his work, Hauerwas consistently emphasizes the
importance of character in the moral life, and of the distinctiveness of a
Christian character. Character is "the qualification of a man's self-
agency through his beliefs, intentions, and actions,"[38] and, correspondingly, a Christian character "is qualified under the form of Christ and
the task he entrusts to us."[39] But though he says that "Christian character is the formation of our *affections* and actions,"[40] Hauerwas concen-
trates almost exclusively on *action* in his description of the Christian
moral life. For example, when he proposes to answer the question,
"Why did she do that?" he writes that

the reason given, if honestly put forward, must in some
sense arise from the kind of person one is. This can be seen

> by the fact that often when we are asked about our actions, the question is not just in reference to the action itself, but is seeking to know why *we* did it as the kinds of persons we are....[41]

Or we read that

> we are profoundly what we do, for once action is understood in its essential connection with our agency it is apparent that by acting we form not merely the act but ourselves in the process.[42]

From within the interactive model, however, we can say that the same kind of training and evaluation of character can take place by discovering what one *is affected by*, or, put in a more theological context, by what one suffers (rather than what one does). The kinds of things that are taken as joyful, appealing, revolting, shameful—that is, our *passions*—disclose "the kinds of persons we are."

Sometimes Hauerwas' own statements point the way for such an understanding of the passions as disclosing our character. We see a suggestion of attention to passions (affections) in his first statement quoted here on Christian character. Then for example, in speaking about the significance of narrative, he says:

> The field of a story is actions (either deeds or dreams) or their opposite, sufferings. In either case, what action or passion is seen to unfold is something we call "character."[43]

Hauerwas' readers will appreciate the weight of the word "story" (or "narrative") there. Its significance for my own work is that narrative not only bears the descriptions (i.e. its "meaning," without which there is no passion), but also because the historical nature of a story corresponds to what I have called the "historical trajectory" of passions toward their finality. But Hauerwas never adequately accounts for passions in his work because his understanding of moral agency is too tied to action, and to self-determination. For example, he writes, "He is self-determining because he can in fact choose between alternative descriptions (and thus action) by which his act is made his own."[44] What he means by "our own" is "to claim [our actions] as crucial to our history."[45] In his speaking of moral agency, Hauerwas seems to be in conflict with his emphasis on community; community, which is so important in his theology, surely must have a stronger role in determining the significance of actions and sufferings than it appears to have in Hauerwas' moral agent.

I believe that the interactive model can reconcile the claims of community and self in Hauerwas' work, because in that model we can *expand the notion of agency.* That is, we can see a moral agent not only as acting, but also as acting *through empowerment by an other.* We express that latter notion of agency when we say, "I am acting as his agent." The interactive model of the passions can sustain that notion because of its understanding of the passions as the self's receiving of value from the other, while retaining its own distinct nature.

That full idea of *agency* (both acting, and acting on behalf of) is fitting for Christian agency, particularly if we are going to model Christian agency on the agency of Jesus himself. For example, Jesus compliments the centurion for his act of faith. If we examine that act of faith more closely, we see that the centurion begins not by recognizing Jesus' power to act, but by recognizing that Jesus is under authority— is an agent of an Other. "I am a man under authority myself," he says, "and I have others under me" (Mt 8:9). Hauerwas himself is alert to this, and quotes Julian Hartt's description of Jesus as "the supreme agent of the Kingdom, agent both in the sense of one who acts and in the sense of one who represents the interests of another."[46] The theological advantage of this full notion of agency lies in its ability to explain that Jesus, and with him all Christians, receive their true power to act inasmuch as they have a passion for God.

We can summarize this theological section by looking again at the activity of Fabian with his little brother. Each day that Fabian visited, he was on his own, and had to rely on his own insights in interaction with the boy. And also, each day he returned to report to, and pray to God with, his Christian community. In his healing of the boy, and especially in his healing of the boy from violence, Fabian was acting as an agent of Jesus, and of our Christian prayer community of "big brothers." We helped him to maintain himself, his otherness to the dossier of abuse in the interaction with his little brother. Put another way, Fabian was a missionary, drawing his little brother into a community where violence had no status, and away from a community where violence had great significance and importance. Finally, the little boy was moved by the same love that first moved Fabian. Finally, the little boy was no longer moved by violence, but by Fabian's embodiment of the love of God.

With these insights from the contemporary scientists, philosophers and theologians, let us turn to the reflections of Thomas Aquinas. I believe he would be happy with the course of our stories and studies so far, since, in Thomas' understanding, we do not entirely move ourselves; we are "moved movers." And both Thomas and Hauerwas would agree:

> The Christian seeks neither autonomy nor independence, but rather to be faithful to the way that manifests the conviction that we belong to another. Thus Christians learn to describe their lives as a gift rather than an achievement.[47]

3.

OVERVIEW OF THE THEOLOGY
OF THOMAS AQUINAS

We come from Allah, and we return to Allah.

—Qur'an

When we study Thomas Aquinas' *Treatise on the Passions* in the next chapter, we will find in it much that aids our effort to give a contemporary moral account of the passions. The *Treatise,* however, is part of a larger work, the *Summa theologiae.*[1] To understand the *Treatise* fully, we need first to discover how it fits into Thomas' theological project, and specifically how it fits in the progress of the *Summa theologiae.* This chapter, then, presents a general overview of Thomas' life and theology, as a background for reading the *Treatise on the Passions.*

I. Thomas Aquinas: A Brief Biography[2]

We are not sure of the exact date of Thomas Aquinas' birth. We know that he was born in the duchy of Aquino, Italy, sometime around 1225. He died when he was only about fifty years old, but he wrote prodigiously, sometimes keeping several scribes busy with texts he was dictating. Besides being an intellectual giant, Thomas was also a great preacher, and people would come from miles around when they heard he was going to preach.

Thomas began to write theology in the same way everyone else did in those days, with a commentary on Peter Lombard's *Sentences.*

As he progressed in his studies, however, he got more involved in what was the great theological challenge of his age. For hundreds of years, after the fall of the Roman empire, the people and scholars of Europe had lost some very important documents of their western intellectual history, most notably the writings of the great Greek philosopher, Aristotle. Those documents *were* kept, however, in Muslim libraries and archives in the Middle East. There, Arabic scholars built up enormous and insightful commentaries on the works of western philosophy.[3] In the west, the Muslim presence in Andalus (Spain) produced a great flowering of culture and learning. In the twelfth century, many Arabic documents from both the east and west of the Islamic Empire were translated into Latin under the sponsorship of Archbishop Raymond of Toledo, and so became available to Christian scholars. With those translations, the Muslim commentator Ibn Rushd (Averroes) had an especially great influence on Christian scholars, some of whom became known as Averroists.[4] The difficulty was that when the western scholars rediscovered thinkers like Aristotle, they got Aristotle *and* the Muslim commentaries.

Western theologians now had a problem. The Muslim scholars saw that everything that they read in the archived western documents reaffirmed the truth of *Islam*.[5] All the theology of the *west,* however, had been based on the presupposition that western thought was intrinsically *Christian* thought. But if Aristotle, one of the founding fathers of western philosophy, was seen to be supporting Islam, then how could theologians think of western thought as properly Christian? This caused a great stir among scholars.

In the east, Muslims had encountered western Christianity in the crusades, and it was not a happy meeting.[6] The Muslim people were only aware that armies of men with horses and broadswords came to attack homes where they had been living in peace for centuries. Why? Something about their pope and their God wanting them to do it. They were therefore not fond of this religion and its God. Their scholars, who were far more advanced than those of the west, began to criticize this religion. Some of those criticisms were sophisticated and others crude, but they all had their effect. Not only the scholars were wondering; people were confused.[7]

Into all of this strode Thomas Aquinas. For the people, he preached popular sermons. For scholars, he wrote the *Summa contra gentiles*, defending Christianity against the attacks of what to him were unbelievers. But he also got into some trouble with his own believing community. That was because Thomas believed that Aristotle, proper-ly read, *could* be used to support Christian thought, and began to write his own commentaries on Aristotle's works. Many church people were understandably suspicious of Aristotle and his "unbeliever's ways." And they were especially suspicious of anyone, like Thomas, who would try to make Aristotle's philosophy the basis for his theology. Yet, in many ways, Thomas thought about *his* faith what the Muslim commentator Ibn Rushd (Averroes) thought about his:

> Since this religion is true and summons to the study which leads to knowledge of the Truth, we the Muslim communi-ty know definitely that demonstrative study does not lead to [conclusions] conflicting with what Scripture [*Qur'an*] has given us; for truth does not oppose truth but accords with it and bears witness to it.[8]

In the years since his death, scholars have increasingly recognized how great Thomas' thought was.[9] In contemporary times, Thomistic studies are having another rebirth, especially among ethicists. I believe that is because the turmoil of his age is so much like our own. Then and now, it seems, we have many differing understandings about right and wrong. Many people have given up trying to meet the challenges of inte-grating new and sometimes conflicting beliefs, and have fallen back on ethical relativism: It's right if it's right for me. We sense that the old structures cannot hold—at least not in the same way as they had before. Perhaps the best modern thinker analyzing this modern conflict of sys-tems is Alasdair MacIntyre. His 1981 book, *After Virtue*, which describes the breakdown of coherency in western philosophy, still influ-ences the thought of most contemporary ethicists. Those ethicists are try-ing to put the pieces together in a new synthesis, just as Thomas did for his time. And they are turning to Thomas to find out how he did it.

One of the ways that Thomas brought unity to all the different, competing claims of right and wrong was to focus on the *body*, and espe-cially on the *passions*. If Thomas' project was to forge a synthesis for his time, he was on really safe ground here. Everyone is embodied; every-one has feelings. And all those feelings have similar bodily changes.

Thomas did not have contemporary scientific studies, of course, but he knew the basics. He knew that all people—Aristotle and Ibn Rushd, believers and unbelievers, sinners and saints—smiled when they were happy, cried when they were sad, gritted their teeth when they were angry.

But in dealing with the body and passions, Thomas was more than just "safe"—he could be inspired. For Thomas also had a *God* who had a body. He had Jesus, who smiled with children, wept with Martha and Mary, and got angry with money changers in God's house. He had Jesus, whose compassion for the leper "hit him in his gut," who was the full revelation of God the Father, whose Spirit was poured out on all humankind. He had his devotion to the eucharist, the body of Christ. There seems to be no better focal point to talk about unity than something in which we all share—even with God: the body and the passions. Dancing just below the surface of the *Treatise on the Passions* is Thomas' wonder at the passionate love that the Father has for the Son who took flesh from Mary. And what compels Thomas to write is his conviction that he—and all of us—are invited *in the flesh* to share in that same passionate love.

I do not want to give the impression that the whole purpose of the *Summa* was to talk about being embodied, and the passions. What Thomas wanted to do in the *Summa theologiae* was what the title said: unify and integrate *all* theology, even that of his opponents, in one grand scheme. But in this book we will concentrate on what Thomas was saying about the body and passions. When we do, I think we will see the *Treatise on the Passions* as a very rich resource for understanding Thomas' theology. We will also see that the *Treatise* is quite congenial to modern scientific studies on the passions. Because of that, Thomas can begin to provide *contemporary* theologians and ethicists with a good intellectual basis for incorporating modern scientific understandings of affectivity into their understandings of God, creation, and human beings. First, though, let us look at the *Summa.*

II. The Structure of the *Summa theologiae*

Thomas intended the *Summa* as a text for people to study before they were ordained. We have already said that Thomas was trying to unify all systems of thought in the *Summa*. Thomas, however, was also pioneering a new form of theology, where every part of that theology relates to every other part, and all of those parts to the whole. That new kind of study is now called *systematics*, or *systematic theology*, and the *Summa* is just such a work.

Thomas puts the whole *Summa* in terms of a discussion. Once you catch the rhythm of it, and perhaps place yourself in the schools and universities where all the debates were raging, and perhaps see Thomas struggling to reject false thinking, draw all the strands of discussion together and unify them into a single systematic statement of truth, the *Summa* is fairly dramatic. It is divided into three major parts. The First Part deals with God, and with creation, which Thomas calls the *exitus*, or "going forth" from God. The Second Part (which is subdivided into two parts) talks about humankind's return (*reditus*) to God. The Second Part (first subdivision) is where our *Treatise on the Passions* is. The Third Part explains the return to God as taught by Christ, that is, the specific Christian return.

Each Part of the *Summa*, each subdivision, each treatise, is put in the form of questions to be discussed, and each question has several sub-questions (called articles) to it. The *Treatise on the Passions*, for example, has twenty-seven questions. Thomas starts with the question, "Is there any passion in the soul?" Immediately three "objectors" speak up. No, they say, and each gives his reason why the soul cannot have passion. But Thomas says Yes, the soul *does* have passions ("Sed contra"), and Look, I can demonstrate for you why this is true. So he quotes from his theological tradition (the scripture, or one of the recognized theologians who preceded him), or from his philosophical tradition (often Aristotle). Then he presents his proof logically (*Responsio*). Finally he responds to the objectors, one by one. Then the *next* sub-question (article) follows from the one just discussed ("Well, if *that's* what you think, then what about...?" "If you think *that*, then don't you *also* have to hold that...?").

The whole *Summa* is structured that way. Thomas has different numbers of questions, of articles, of objectors, but the format is always the same, and the logical progression from question to question is always the same. It is something like a dialogue with all points of view represented, and each person arguing his point of view as forcefully as possible. Starting with the very first question in the very first Part of the *Summa,* Thomas begins to weave everything together in one grand and dramatic statement about God and God's creatures. Let us begin, then, at the beginning of the *Summa,* and find out what Thomas says about God.

III. In the Beginning, God

Thomas begins the *Summa* by saying that you cannot say anything about God.[10] That may sound strange: why is Thomas writing all this theology about God if he cannot say anything about God? But Thomas is right. Our finite minds can never really grasp God, who is infinite. We cannot even talk about a *part* of God, because God has no parts. It is an all or nothing proposition, really, and Thomas logically has to choose nothing.

Thomas, however, learned something significant about God from this defeat of his language. Why *can't* we talk about God even in part? Because, as we have said, God has no parts (the theological statement is: God is simple). Why *can't* we say anything about God? Because our words are really physical things, while God is Spirit. Why *can't* our language grasp God? Because God is infinite. Why *can't* we describe God? Because when we describe anything, we describe it by comparing it to other things. And God is incomparable: incomparably wise, incomparably just, incomparably merciful, incomparably compassionate, incomparably wonderful, incomparably loving, lovely, and lovable. All of a sudden, it seems Thomas has a great deal to say about God.

There are three other things which Thomas accomplishes by that marvelous assertion that we cannot say anything about God. First, Thomas honors the mystic tradition. All my reading of Thomas' theology, and all my reading of his biographies, convince me that Thomas was a true mystic. He belonged to an order, the Dominicans, whose express purpose it was to take the fruits of their *prayer* and present it by preaching to the people. And it seems that the core of mystic prayer is the utter incomprehensibility of God. Put another way, God is the ultimate other. A modern mystic, Thomas Merton, once described his own mystical experience of encountering God. "You can't say anything about it," he wrote. "The only thing you can do is point to every-

thing you know and say, 'It's not that. It's not that.'" That was
Thomas' experience, the encounter he wanted, for all his intellectual
prowess, to honor: God is incomparable, immeasurable, incomprehen-
sible, simply wonderful.

Second, Thomas wanted to honor what we call revelation. We
cannot really comprehend God, so God reveals God's self to us. This
revelation comes to us through scripture and the teachings that the
church calls "revealed." Of course the principal revelation of God for
Thomas was Jesus the Christ, come in the flesh. Over the years, reflection on the mystery of the incarnation of Christ led the church to the
development of the doctrine of the Trinity. Thomas is saying that you
can not arrive at, or conclude to, such understandings of incarnation and
Trinity by a process of intellectual investigation, or logical analysis.
What Thomas is really honoring, then, is faith. His Christian faith allows
him to say certain things about God which are true, because God reveals
them as true. I want especially to draw attention to the revelation of the
nature of God as Trinity. The presence of God permeates the whole
Summa, and it is a Trinitarian presence. We will find echoes of that
Trinitarian belief when we study the *Treatise on the Passions* as well.

Thomas has a third, and most important, reason for saying that
our intellectual tools and abilities come second when it comes to
knowing God. Thomas wants to acknowledge that God is Love, that
the best way to know God is not by the mind, but through the heart.
That conviction, that God is Love, permeates the whole *Summa*.
Understanding that theme is vitally important if we wish to understand
what Thomas is saying specifically about the body and passions in the
Treatise on the Passions.

IV. God's Creatures: The *Exitus* and the *Reditus*

After his opening discussion of God, Thomas turns to God's creation, going forth from God. Again, he is conscious that God is Love,
and that God is Trinity. In the very self of God, there is love, genera-
tivity, and mutual sharing. From that Love, the Trinity creates. Even
though God is not compelled, there is a certain inevitability that such
Love would also create so as to share Love with creatures. Thomas
sees that as the purpose for all creatures: that they share in the Love

that is God, since God has created all creatures out of the very fabric, as it were, of God's own self. Thomas means *all* creatures. Rocks, trees, air, fire, animals and vegetables, human beings and spirit-beings—all are good in that they were created and are being constantly kept in their existence by God who is good.[11] God shares God's love and being with each and all of them in the form of their simply existing, and, even more, in the uniqueness of their existence. Put concretely, the tree outside the window of the room where I am writing is a tree because God is present to it in a "tree way." God is constantly present to trees in their treeness—even more wonderfully, in their oakness, or pineness or mapleness.[12] What sustains a creature in its uniqueness is the unique way that God is present to that creature. God also sustains the human *soul*—that which makes us to be who we are—with a unique presence. In the *Summa*, then, Thomas systematically works out the implications of Augustine's statement, "God is more interior to me than my inmost self."

God creates, then, for love, so that creatures too can be loved and love. Now I want to return to the Trinity for a moment. Surely this is not the place to discuss all the wonders of Trinitarian theology. But let us look at just one aspect of that theology. God is Love, and God is Trinity. Each Person of the Trinity is completely distinct, but at the same time is in total communion and intimacy with each other. If God is Love, and God is Trinity, it must therefore be true that both of those things, distinctness and communion, are necessary in love. So Thomas sees that interplay between distinctiveness (individuality) and community as necessary for all Love's creatures as well. This is how Thomas understands creation. By creating, God individuated; God, as it were, set each creature apart so that each could be its distinct self. But each creature is a distinct, individual being precisely so that the creature can be in communion, can love and be loved, most especially by God. Otherwise, creation would be abandonment, and individuality would be pathology. By the same act, then, that God calls creatures into being, God calls them into love.

Who is the greatest Love? God. To fulfill its true nature, then, to satisfy fully the very purpose of its being, the creature must be caught up in the love of God, loving and being loved. Now the progression of the first part of the *Summa* becomes more clear. First, in creation, God, as it were, sets the creature apart. Second, inasmuch as the creature

continues to be, the creature is already sharing in God, because God is
the one who continuously keeps all beings in existence. Third, God
also calls the creature to "return" for the fulfillment of its being.
"Everything there is," writes Paul in his letter to the Romans, "comes
from God and is caused by God and exists for God" (11:36). For
Thomas, the story of the created world is salvation history. The drama
of the journey of creatures back to God, their happiness pervades the
whole *Summa.*

In Thomas' understanding of the creation, the sustaining, and the
return then, we can see the reflection of the Father, the Spirit and the
Son in the Trinity. Now let us turn our thoughts in a different direction.
In the "return" of all creatures to the bosom of the One who created
them, we can hear echoes of the return of the prodigal son who appreciated the love of his father precisely because he had been away. These
reflections may seem to be digressions in our outlining of the *Summa,*
but thinking in totalities is the nature, and the beauty, of Thomas' systematic theology. For him, the whole world was, in the words of
Hopkins, "charged with the grandeur of God." Throughout the *Summa,*
even while he seems to be discussing something else, we can see glis-
tenings and gleamings of the love of the One in whom all things in
heaven and on earth were created (Col 1:16).

Let us continue our outline of the *Summa.* We have already seen
the dynamics of the creation and return (the *exitus* and the *reditus*) in
the love that characterize all creatures. When Thomas examines creation, then, he can never simply look at it in and of itself. He must
always look at its individuality, its need for relationship, and its *final
goal* (Thomas calls it the "end"; modern ethicists sometimes still use
the Greek word *telos*) of return to God. From his earliest writings, we
see that Thomas understands a creature's need for both individuality
and relatedness. In his commentary on the third book of Peter
Lombard's *Sentences,* Thomas "begins with the general observation
that in all things there are to be found two sorts of perfection, one by
which the thing *subsists in itself,* the other by which it is *ordered to
other things...proportionate to itself.*"[13]

We have to keep two things in mind here. First, those two ways
that a creature is perfectible are interrelated: creatures need relationships to be fully individuated, and need to be individuated in order to
be in relationships with others, and both are the dynamics of love. It is

something like breathing out and breathing in—you need both. We have already seen another way to say this: creatures are *constitutively interrelational.* That is to say, what makes a creature to be what it is—what *constitutes* it—is relationships. Second, the creature increases its perfection—its distinctness *and* its relatedness—as the creature returns closer to God, who is perfect Love. That is the final goal (*telos*) of creation and of each creature.

Keeping those two things in mind, we can understand what Thomas means when he says that a creature is "ordered" to other creatures. Thomas observed that creatures are drawn to approach (attracted to) others of their own kind. For Thomas, it was not opposite, but similar things that attracted. Dewan, in the above quote, says that certain others are "proportionate" for a thing. Thomas himself used that and other words to convey the same sense, such as "fitting," "congruent," "proper," "apt," "inclined," "disposed toward," and "connatural." Thomas noticed that chickens are drawn to approach other chickens. They also avoid chicken hawks. So that is part of the ordering of creatures: creatures are drawn to approach others which promote their existence, and thus avoid others who harm that existence. We saw in Chapter 1 that research has revealed that living organisms have a nature which requires physical, bonding interaction with a living other, usually a similar organism, who is significant to that organism. Thomas saw all this approaching and avoiding as the activity of a creation being called toward its final goal: fulfillment in God. God is calling all creation into communion with God, which means greater life, greater individuation, greater community—in a word, greater love. God is, in the fullest sense of the word, *attractive* to all creatures.

From that perspective, then, each creature *is* called, *is* drawn, *is moved* by God, the ultimate other, through all the others of creation. All the movement that we see in the world finds its origin in the call of God to final communion. Movement *toward* that greater love (approach) necessarily means movement *away* from (avoiding) others which would be unfitting for the creature's God-supported existence. Thomas saw that movement of approach and avoidance as characterizing all creation, even inanimate things. He noticed that rocks are drawn to approach the earth, which is a more fitting place for them than the air. In their being drawn to approach the earth, they avoid the upper reaches of the air. Fire is the opposite. It "loves" the air and is always trying to approach it. If you try to keep it down, say, by covering it, it will resist you. If you succeed, you will have violated its existence (notice: by cutting it off from its proper or fitting relationships with another) so completely that you will smother and destroy it.

Why is that important? Thomas is writing systematic theology, so he wants everything to relate to everything else. He wants to relate that rock, being drawn back to its "natural home," the earth, to salvation history. This is how he does it. Thomas says that, when you separate the rock from its natural home, you have by so doing created a "natural desire" between the rock and the earth. It is as though that space between the rock and the earth were filled with mutual attractiveness, a "natural longing," the earth attracting, calling to the rock, as it were, and the rock yearning to return. That mutual, natural longing remains unsatisfied as long as you obstruct it by holding on to the rock. Once you release the rock, it naturally returns to what has been drawing it—that thing for which it had a "natural passion"—the earth. Then, having satisfied its natural passion (and, necessarily, the requirements of divine order), the rock can rest.

In Thomas' systematic thinking, a similar dynamic holds true for human beings. God's creation of us as distinct beings, God's setting us apart from God's self, creates at the same time a passion for God in our very being. We naturally long for God. We yearn for God as a rock naturally desires to be reunited with the earth. We hunger for God as a fire hungers for air. The psalmist says, "O God, my soul yearns for you, like a dry, weary land without water." And once our impediments (sins) are taken away, once we are set free, we naturally rush to our "rest" in God's arms, like that stone, rushing back to earth after we release it— like the prodigal son returning to his father's embrace. "You have made us for Yourself," said Augustine, Thomas' predecessor, "and our hearts are restless, until they rest in You." In the *Summa,* and especially in the *Treatise on the Passions,* Thomas is systematically working out what that means for humans, and for all the created order.

V. *Appetitus* in General

Being drawn to approach certain things and consequently avoiding other things is part of the "natural equipment" of all creatures for

Thomas. Thomas has a special name for that dynamic. He called it *appetitus* (ap-pet-EE-tus). I want to leave the word in its Latin form for several reasons. We could perhaps translate that as "appetite," "desire," or, better, "inclination." But we have a problem with all those English words. They connote a sense of movement *toward* (approach) but not the sense of movement *away from* (avoidance). The Latin word *appetitus* means *both* being drawn toward, and consequent movement away from, both approach and necessary avoidance, both desire and repugnance. We do not have one English word that does that, so we are going to keep the Latin *appetitus* in this book.[14] This dual sense of the word *appetitus* also presents Thomas as open to the Darwinian insight we spoke of in Chapter 1: that the fundamental and simple roots of all affectivity lies in approach and avoidance.[15] We will also keep the word *appetitus* as a kind of shorthand reminder for our understanding of *movement* in the *Summa*: for Thomas, to say "nature" is to say "natural movement," or *appetitus*.[16] Finally, and most importantly for this book, our possible English translations of *appetitus* all seem to convey the sense of something self-generated toward the other. For Thomas, *appetitus* is primarily *other*-generated. We *are* drawn by, *are* attracted by or repelled by, and in each case *are moved* by the *other*, in Thomas' view. That also serves his purpose of systematic unity. That is, Thomas focuses on the other in *all* his accounts of *appetitus,* and that allows him always to maintain his emphasis on the primacy of the ultimate Other throughout the story of creation. And of course, such an understanding of the *appetitus* as ultimately grounded in the attractiveness of God will be essential for his *Treatise on the Passions*. With that understanding, Thomas can explain exactly what it means to have passions "in the right way, at the right time, toward the right person," etc. It means to have all our passions ordered by the governing passion of creation; it means to have a passion for God.

VI. Natural, Sensate, and Intellective *Appetitus*

Thomas divides *appetitus* into three levels according to freedom of movement and level of participation in the divine reason which orders the universe. He calls these three levels the natural (physical),

sensate (cognitional), and intellective (rational) *appetitus*. Let us look
at each of them briefly.

When he speaks of natural (physical) *appetitus*, Thomas is usually referring to what we would call inanimate things, things that have no
senses, things that are wholly subject to time and space, such as the
rocks and the fire we were speaking of earlier. When, for example, you
pick up a rock and release it, it falls. We would attribute that to gravity; Thomas would call it natural *appetitus*. The rock has a natural
appetitus against the air, and a natural *appetitus* for the earth. In that, it
partakes (unknowingly, of course) in the divine reason which gives
order to the universe.

In the rock's return to earth, Thomas, as we have seen, also perceives a pattern for the return of all creatures to their home in God.
Thus natural *appetitus* fits into his overall understanding of the purpose for all creation. Thomas, however, does not consider natural
appetitus in and of itself as a matter of morality. That is because sheerly physical things do not move themselves, they are moved. A more
colorful way of saying the same thing would be to say that rocks have
no choices, no freedom. They are bound to stay where they are placed,
or to move according to the natural order. Similarly the human being,
being physical, also partakes in natural *appetitus* (we would fall if
dropped[17]). But that feature of our existence, in and of itself, is not a
matter of morality for Thomas, since morality involves *choices*. We
cannot choose not to fall, so Thomas does not consider the morality of
natural *appetitus* in and of itself.[18]

But that qualification "in and of itself" is important for Thomas.
If we leap from a high place, that is a matter of choice, and so of
morality. Negatively, we can imagine someone joining a cult or any
group where he had no choices, where he only had to "follow orders."
In that case, depriving the person of choice would be violating his status as a moral being. A person cannot properly even volunteer for such
a demotion of status. From Thomas' point of view, such activity could
be seen as a violation of the created order, since such a person would
be behaving more like a rock than a human being. Compulsion violates
the nature of a moral creature.

Thomas distinguishes another level of *appetitus*, above natural
appetitus. He calls it "sensate *appetitus*," and by that he means creatures that have sense-perception—animals. I believe that the activity of

animals always impressed Thomas. He could watch a bird building a nest, or observe a cat stalking a bird, or see a dog jump with delight at the return of its caretaker, and he knew that something very significant, beyond the necessities of natural *appetitus*, was going on. He explained that "something beyond" by saying that animals have a spiritual reality as well as a physical one. Animals have animal souls. Like rocks and other creatures with natural *appetitus*, animals can *be moved* since they have bodies (they would fall if dropped). But because of their spiritual qualities, animals can *move themselves*, as rocks and other things which only have natural *appetitus* cannot. Sensate *appetitus* is characterized by freedom and choice; animals partake of the divine reason and order in a better way than inanimate things.

When Thomas presents us with sensate *appetitus*, several powerful insights converge. He expressly associates the presence of a spiritual reality with freedom. For creatures, that spiritually grounded freedom takes the form of some kind of *choice* about their movements, and intention about their immediate goals. But also, when spiritual reality is united with physical reality, we find powers of *sense-perception,* which rocks and fire do not have. So Thomas sees the three—spirit, sense-perception, and choice—as bound together. Think of a cat stalking a bird. Eyes, nose, ears, whiskers, are all engaged in pursuing that goal. Without those, the cat could not stalk, and could not even intend to stalk the bird. If the cat's senses were confused (Thomas would say, "not in order") the cat could not stalk the bird. But with its sense-perception, the cat has a certain amount of freedom: the cat can stalk the bird or not; it can stalk this or that bird; it can give up if the bird is unreachable. So when Thomas saw that a creature had sense-perception, he knew that it also had spiritual capabilities, like choice and intention.[19] The reverse is also true. The fact that a physical creature had choice and intention must mean that it also had senses.

The last few sentences of the previous paragraph show something else about Thomas' thought. When Thomas thought about animals as beings made up of spirit and matter, he saw the sensate soul as embracing the whole physical reality (and natural *appetitus*) of the animal. He did not think of animals as matter to which a spirit has been "added," as though there were two separate realities. Nor did he conceive of the sensate soul acting on the body as though the body were an external object of some kind. The sensate soul permeates, or suffuses—or, best, animates the whole physical reality of the animal. So a whole new species, an ensouled species, is created by God with powers beyond that of merely natural *appetitus*. For Thomas, even though we can consider such a composite (composed of body and soul) creature and its powers from different aspects, the creature itself must finally be understood as a *totality*.

In Thomas' discussion of animals, we can see a value for our discussion of the morality of human passions. We recall from Chapter 1 that one of the ways that we begin to recover our moral agency is to "come to our senses"—our physical senses, like touch and sight and smell. Thomas would surely be open to that understanding, since, for him, spiritual realities like freedom and choice are intimately bound up with physical senses. We can also understand why Thomas is so insistent on the importance of the human body in his account of the morality of the passions.

The more spiritual a thing is, the less it is necessarily moved by another, and the more it can move itself and other things. The summit and source of all this motion is God, who is pure Spirit, and the Unmoved Mover.[20] Sheerly physical things, like rocks, in their distance from God, do not move themselves. Composite beings, such as animals, are closer to the Divine Being because they are ensouled; they can move themselves and other creatures. But the *appetitus* of animals (sensate *appetitus*) still suffers from its distance from God, and the fact that all its perception is bound to bodily organs. That is, animals cannot know what is beyond their senses. Since animal souls are so bound up with their bodies, their freedom is limited. Our cat, for example, cannot choose to fast from food. Therefore, in the final analysis, animals are more moved than moving, more bound than free.[21] And we can also see that if we as humans are fixed solely on what our senses perceive, we would be less than what we are created to be. We would be more bound than free.

The highest level of *appetitus* Thomas calls "intellective *appetitus*," and he begins his discussion of it with his *Treatise on the Angels*. He keeps those same principles of *appetitus*—freedom, participation in divine reason, and movement—and imagines how they would apply in the case of pure spirit-beings. The result is an exercise in sheer intellectual joy. Thomas is called "The Angelic Doctor," and when you watch his intellect soar with the angels, it is easy to see why. When he discusses the freedom of the angels, Thomas reminds us that angels have no physical body; they are pure spirit, and so are most like God in creation. That means, in Thomas' world view, that they are the most free of all beings. They are of course attracted by goodness, but they are never bound by compulsion; they are not moved by any exterior force; they do everything by their own free choice, and according to God's ordering of creation.

In one place in the *Treatise on the Angels*, Thomas is defending the traditional understanding that Michael cast Lucifer out of heaven. His objectors say that such a deed would have been impossible, since Michael, "only" an archangel, was not as powerful as Lucifer, who was of a higher "choir." Thomas responds that Michael *could* defeat Lucifer because Michael remained in communion with God, and so had infinite resources for the battle, while Lucifer, who had separated from God, was "left to his own, not inconsiderable, natural power." Again, I invite the reader to "digress," and reflect on that explanation in the context of our common struggle to live a moral life. We could strive on our own power, but we would fail. If we remain in interaction with God, however, we have inexhaustible resources for overcoming any obstacle, and for attaining our goal. Thus Thomas is saying theologically what Isaiah had discovered long ago: "Young men may grow tired and weary, youths may stumble and fall, but those who hope in the Lord renew their strength. They shall mount up on wings like eagles; they shall run and not grow weary, they shall walk and not grow faint" (Is 40:30-31). Even in the *Treatise on the Angels* then, Thomas shows us the value of having an ongoing passion for God.

We need to leave the spirit-beings, however, and proceed to Thomas' study of the *appetitus* of human beings. Human beings also have intellective *appetitus*, but human beings are unique in that that intellect is united (Thomas would say, "composite") with a physical reality. As composite of both body and spirit, we are moved movers,[22] as are the animals. Our having a rational (intellective) soul, however, means that our way of perceiving is *not* entirely bound by our senses— human beings can know things beyond sense experience. We are able, in a basic way, to perceive the Supreme Good. Like the angels, our *appetitus* is drawn by God, and we are therefore able to order all our particular goods in light of the Supreme Good. That is why Thomas *begins* his discussion of human beings with a discussion of the *final goal*, union with God (I.75-82). That particular plan of presentation fits the general scheme of the *Summa*. Also, by beginning with a focus on the other, Thomas presents us with a consistent account of the three levels of *appetitus*. The rock, with its natural *appetitus*, cannot help but fall back to earth. The cat, with its sensate *appetitus*, is more free to choose, but its intention is bound by its own physical needs. For its part, intellective *appetitus* cannot help but be attracted by the loveliness of God. Thomas here agrees with Aristotle: "Happiness is what all people seek." And for Thomas, the supreme happiness, the final goal which the intellective *appetitus* perceives and is drawn by, is union with God.

We need to make a point here, similar to one we made earlier. We have often heard Thomas' definition of the human being as a rational animal. Thomas does not mean to say that we have a body into which a soul is inserted. We are not "fallen angels"—intellective souls placed into physical bodies. Nor are we, on the other hand, animals to which an intellect has been added. Recall what Thomas said about animal (sensate) *appetitus* in relation to natural *appetitus*. The same is true in the case of the intellective *appetitus*. As a composite of body and intellective soul, the human being is a completely different species. The intellective power of the soul suffuses or permeates—or, better, animates—the whole composite being.[23] When speaking of animals, Thomas would say that the new level of being, and the new capability of movement, was characterized and ordered by *instinct*.[24] When speaking of human beings, Thomas says that this new level of being and new capability of movement is characterized and ordered by *rationality*. Thomas surely considers physical movement as part of his description of what it means to be a human being. But what is most characteristic of humans is movement in accord with their rational *appetitus*. And that rational *appetitus* is drawn directly by the Supreme Good, and so is able to see the final goal of union with God. That vision of the Supreme Good, and the power to act on it, is characteristic of rationality. Therefore, rational beings partake in divine ordering of the universe in a better way—not "blindly" as rocks or animals do. Partaking by rational beings is more properly called participation. That is one way that Thomas sees our role as rational beings: we are to participate in the ordering of all the universe back toward God, our happiness and goal.[25]

Thomas insists on the integrated nature of the human being. The human being is a body-sensate-intellective totality. In our first chapter, we called it "the organic unity of the moral agent." "Even though the soul is a part of the human body," Thomas wrote, "it is not the total human being, and my soul is not my self."[26]

VII. Rationality in the Moral Project

Thomas' insistence on the organic unity of the soul and body of the human being is central for understanding the project of the *Summa,* and crucial for understanding the significance of his *Treatise on the Passions.* He says that anything that we claim to be true about the human being (like rationality, for example) is true of the whole human being.[27] Thomas shares the same vision of the human being that we discovered in our discussion of the body in Chapter 1. Thomas would agree that the body shares in rationality. He would also agree that evaluation is characteristic of the entire embodied organism. We have called that feature, the *organic unity* of the agent. For Thomas, that means that the lower powers of the human being (like physical movement, or hunger) are already ordered toward rationality from our conception.[28] When theologians discuss the nature of Christian salvation, they say that we are "already-but-not-yet" saved. Similarly, for Thomas, the human being is "already-but-not-yet" a rational animal.[29] That is why he uses the word "composite" in referring to such beings. We must be careful in our use of words like "integrated," or even "organic unity," because they carry a sense that the full unity of the moral agent is complete. When we use "composite," or "organic unity," we need to keep in mind both senses of already and not-yet, since that is what Thomas wants.

The lifelong moral project of a human being would thus be to complete and fulfill the integration of the self, so that the whole self becomes fully rational. I hesitate as I write these words, because of our modern sense of the word "rational." We have images from Descartes of the intellect or our "thinking part" warring against the passions. But the fact that Thomas says that all dimensions of the human being are ordered toward rationality forbids us from using the model of "the intellect against the lower passions." Perhaps it will help to recall what

Thomas means by "rational." It means seeing and being drawn by the
Supreme Good. In fact, if we recall how Thomas began his discussion
of God (with the inadequacy of intellect), we can see that the primary
way of being drawn to God in the first place is *not* by what we would
call exclusively "the intellect," or "thinking." It is the dynamic of
wanting, of desiring, which is most properly and best drawn to God.
That "wanting" is very much analogous to the stone being drawn to the
earth. That is why Thomas can write, "The natural inclination in those
things devoid of reason makes manifest the natural inclination belong-
ing to the will of an intellectual nature" (I.60.5). On a rational level,
the "natural attraction" we have for God's own Self, the rational
appetitus, Thomas calls the Will. The will of the human being is a free
will not just because it can choose its actions (as does an animal), but
because it is called by God (like the people of the exodus) to enjoy the
ultimate freedom of God's own homeland. That, then, is the moral project for Thomas: to move from the seeds of rationality placed in us, to
the full freedom of the sons and daughters of God.

We can summarize Thomas' understanding of the moral project
a different way. As a sensate being, we are, like the animals, drawn to
particular goods, perceptible to our senses. As rational beings, we are
drawn to the Supreme Good, whose loveliness attracts us. As integrated beings, we must see each particular good in light of the Supreme
Good, and to enjoy the Supreme Good in every particular good.[30]
Thomas sees this project not just as personally integrative, but also as
interactive. All others are good (in that they exist) and all good is
attractive to us. We must order all those others such that they are
aligned with the vision of God's goodness. The point of the *Treatise on
the Passions* is to discuss those particular attractions, those senses of
being moved, those experiences of passion, in light of the great drama
of the *Summa*—the journey home to God.

As we draw to the conclusion of this chapter, let us consider matters more directly related to the *Treatise on the Passions*. The first is
another question of translation. Thomas uses the words "subject" (*subjectum*) and "object" (*objectum*) in the *Treatise*. They are roughly
equivalent to what we have been calling "the self" and "the other(s)" in
this book. Thomas' term "subject" has a disadvantage, however, for
the modern reader, since we tend to hear "subject-object" with a
Cartesian overtone, and so think about a subject acting on an object in

a kind of crude action-reaction way. That, as we shall see, is not at all Thomas' understanding of the passions, though surely some have taken him that way.[31] In fact, I hope to show that Thomas' understanding of the passions is far more *interactive* than his commentators have grasped. And I also hope to show that Thomas' understanding of passions is quite congenial to contemporary biochemical and neurophysiological research, from which we have drawn this book's interactive model of the passions. I want to be as faithful to Thomas' insights on integrity and interactivity as I can, while attempting to rescue him from a Cartesian understanding. That is why I will translate Thomas' *subjectum* as "self" or "subject pole." I will translate Thomas' *objectum* as "other" or "object pole."

The next few points are technical, but important if we are going to understand the *Treatise on the Passions*. Thomas says that we take the other in two ways. First, we take the other according to the intellect. Thomas says that the intellect apprehends the other according to the intellect's own mode. That means that the intellect makes its own model of the other, in order to understand it. Simply put, we say, "Oh I know. It's like...." We saw this before, when we saw Thomas talking about the intellect's grasp of God. The intellect cannot grasp God, because God is not *like* anything or anybody. The second way we take the other is according to the will (intellective *appetitus*). In the will, the soul is ordered to the other *as the other is in itself*.[32] The *appetitus* of any creature is drawn to the *good* of the being of any other creature. That mode of apprehension is therefore concerned with uniting with, or avoiding, the other in the right way, at the right time, etc. Again, this is simply Thomas' theological way of maintaining that we are drawn more, and more accurately, by love than by knowledge.

Here is what I also hope to show during our discussion on the *Treatise on the Passions*. When Thomas says "object," he doesn't mean that we look at a thing "objectively" in the Cartesian sense of the word, as though it were an independent object to be observed by an independent observer. For Thomas, objects are constitutively interrelational. So when Thomas says that the will takes the other "as it is in itself," he means to include *how the other is affecting the self* in that description. Thomas' technical way of putting this is to say that the other's *form* (which gives individual identity to the other) affects the self.[33] We still have this sense in English, because we say that something "con-forms" to something else, or we say that something is "trans-formed."

We began this chapter by saying that we could not understand the *Treatise on the Passions* without at least a general overview of the *Summa,* since each part was related to every other part, and every part was related to the whole. Now that we have had that overview, we will find that an interesting thing has happened. When we study the *Treatise on the Passions* in the next chapter, we will see that it is a kind of miniature *Summa,* with most of the themes we have already seen here. Just as each individual part of the *Summa* can only be understood in light of the whole, so the whole can be seen in each individual part. Like Hamlet's play-within-a-play, the *Treatise* will bring special clarity and refinement to the dynamics already present in the drama of the *Summa.* It will help us understand how, when Fabian was moved by the plight of his abused little brother, he was, in the final analysis, moved by a passion for God.

4.

THE *TREATISE ON THE PASSIONS*

You know, and do not know,
what it is to act or suffer.
You know, and do not know,
that action is suffering,
and suffering action.
　　　—T.S. Eliot, *Murder in the Cathedral*

The very length of Thomas' *Treatise on the Passions* shows how important he thinks the passions are for his theology. The *Treatise* runs for 27 Questions[1] in the *Summa*, three full volumes in the *Blackfriars* text and translation that we are using. Of course we cannot do full justice to such a long work here. But if we study some of the major points of the *Treatise* with a knowledge of the interactive model and our overview of the *Summa* as a background, we will grasp Thomas' intent quite well. Throughout the *Treatise*, Thomas speaks about the morality of the passions. For him, that translates to speaking about the rationality of passions, since to be rational is to be passionate. I believe that we will find his account of rational, moral, human passions to be very rich. I believe we will also see how open Thomas is to interpretation within contemporary discussions on the morality of the passions.

I. The Body

The very first Question on the passions (22.1) debates "Whether or not there can be a passion in the soul." In defending his affirmative position, Thomas establishes themes to which he will return again and again in the *Treatise*. He writes:

> We call it "passion" when something is drawn toward some thing as to an agent. However, whatever moves away from that which is fitting for it, is most clearly seen to be drawn to something alien to itself. We can conceive of the passions of the soul even in the mind, which can be thought of as "suffering" (*pati*) when it is sensing or understanding. But properly speaking passions (such that we "suffer the loss" of something) exist only according as there is bodily transmutation. Therefore, when we speak of the passions of the *soul*, we mean that the soul experiences passions only accidentally, inasmuch as it is composite (organically unified) with the body.[2]

Let us examine some of the themes in this opening statement.

Most dramatic is Thomas' statement of why passions are so crucial in the moral life. First, they are in the soul—the very thing that makes us who we uniquely are. We are by nature (being creatures in need of perfection) always being moved by some other. Thomas here indicates that when a creature withdraws from that which is most fitting for that creature, that creature can become something alien to itself. We all know, and some of us have experienced, this scary situation. Something makes us so angry or frightened, or we have indulged so much in an addiction, that we act in a way that is completely out of character. Sometimes we even say, "She was not herself," or, "That was the drink talking." Later in the same question, Thomas makes a further point that this "becoming alien to oneself" increases as the movement of passion increases—as it repeats, or becomes *habitual*. Because passions are in the soul, persistence in such a passion leads to disfigurement of the soul—a deforming of the very identity of an individual (cf. 22.1ad3). Shakespeare gives us a dramatic example of this deforming of humanity in *King Lear*. At the end of the play, Lear carries in the body of his dead daughter, Cordelia, and cries out against his companions, "Oh, you are men of stone!" Those are the moral stakes in the passions: we can become insensate (like stones), or brutal (in its original sense), or humane. Even more, for Thomas, we can become "holy as Christ was holy."

Second, Thomas insists on a most important point here in the beginning, and throughout the *Treatise*: one cannot have passions, properly speaking, without what he calls "bodily transmutation" (*transmutationem corporalem*). Thomas means that in its most common sense: shaking with fear, weeping in sorrow, melting with love.[3] Those "bodily transmutations" or "bodily changes" are essential to understanding the passions, and especially for understanding Thomas' action theory. We saw from Chapter 2 that Motivationists/Cognitivists always have a problem explaining how we go from perception to action. Such a problem simply does not occur for Thomas. According to Thomas, to be in passion means to have bodily changes (blushing, clenching, higher heartbeat, etc.), and those bodily changes are the very material of our perception of the other. Therefore, when we are in passion we are already in some kind of action, since the body is already in act *by the very fact of the self's being in passion to the other.* That is why he can write, "The *appetitus* faculty is said to be more active because it is more the principle of exterior action. But that very activity arises by virtue of the fact that the *appetitus* faculty is more passive, inasmuch as it is ordered to the thing as it is in itself" (22.2ad2). And the action of the passions is already, though primitively, ordered toward approach or avoidance of the other. We heat up in anger in readiness to attack, we experience the sinking feeling of fear to prepare our feet to flee. Darwin would have appreciated this. Thomas knows that those bodily changes are purposive, since evaluation is, as we have already seen, a feature of the entire embodied organism. Therefore, when we look at our bodies in the relationship between the other and the self, we see that the self both is moved, and moves itself in the passions.[4] In Thomas' action theory, the question is not how to get from perception to act. It is *how to have passions in the right way,* so that we approach what it is fitting for us to approach, and avoid what is unfitting.

II. The Other as Agent

When Thomas discusses the relationship between the self and the other, he calls the other an "agent"—a term meaning "the one who is responsible for the action."[5] In the early part of the *Treatise on the Passions,* Thomas chooses to concentrate on the morality—even the agency—of the *other* in the relationship between self and other. This, as we have seen, fits his systematic commitment, since all things begin with the ultimate Other, who is God. He wants to continue to employ this model to describe *all* relationships. So in the same way that he began the *Summa* with God, he begins the *Treatise on the Passions* with the other. In his schema, the self is being moved by the other, which is responsible for the action. Though Thomas is committed to that description of the relationship from the beginning, surely he cannot mean that the self is completely at the mercy of the other. Then *we* would have no responsibility for our actions. So Thomas begins to explain *how*, and to what extent, the other is responsible for the action of the self. He begins by saying that the goodness of the other attracts our *appetitus*, since the *appetitus* is drawn to a thing *as it is in itself.*[6] Thomas says that the *good* of the object pole "creates a certain aptitude or inclination or connaturality for that good in the *appetitus* of the subject pole, and that this pertains to love (*amor*)" (23:4).

Imagine you are working on a hot day in Appalachia, building houses. Someone comes up the ladder carrying a frosty glass. "Do you want some lemonade?" "I'd *love* some!" That is *exactly* what Thomas is talking about. He would say that that lemonade is drawing you to it; he would say it is creating in you an aptitude for itself. Of course, you have a thirst, but Thomas does not want to talk about you just now—he wants to talk about the lemonade.[7] He carefully says that this desire in you *pertains* to love, because when you think about it, the word "love" is a bit out of place here. In one sense, it is right: the focus and organization of your mental and physical powers toward getting that glass of lemonade (knowing how it will conform to the *appetitus* that is your thirst!) looks a lot like love. But the lemonade, though it is in interaction with you (its fitting goodness is drawing you to it), is not really loving you back (cf. 26.4, "Sed Contra"). When he later speaks more of *mutual* attraction (interaction in a more complete sense), Thomas will say that the congruency or aptitude created by the other in the self *is* love (25.2).

In the *Treatise*, then, love begins and ends everything, as it does throughout the *Summa*. The other gives to the self an inclination or aptitude (called "love") so that the self will tend toward the other. If the self is not in the proper place for communion with the other, the other creates a movement toward itself. Once the other and the self are in real union (cf. 25.2 and 25.3), the self experiences delightful or joyful love in the other (23.4).

But what if you are thirsty and no one offers you anything to drink? Now you have a different relationship—because, Thomas would say, you have a *different other*; because a different object pole is moving the subject pole. Now you are not in relationship with "easy-to-attain-lemonade," you are in relationship with "hard-to-attain-lemonade." Thomas, keeping to his position that the other determines the passion in the self, says that each of those two different others gives you different kinds of passion. Thomas says that if you are relating to an "easy-to-attain" other, you have "concupiscible" passions, and if to a "hard-to-attain" other, you have "irascible" passions of the *appetitus.*

We need not spend too much time on the categories of concupiscible and irascible passions. They are not difficult to comprehend, because we already know about Thomas' concerns with movement toward union in the *Summa.*[8] Thomas gives us one way to understand them. He asks us to think of the irascible passions as "between" the concupiscible passions. There is the initial experience of fittingness ("Would I like some lemonade!"), the "between experience" of struggle to attain (hope to get lemonade, boldness of movement down ladder to house to make lemonade), and then the fitting union again (delight of drinking lemonade). Concupiscible passions (easy-to-attain lemonade), then, are love and desire (at the beginning), and delight and joy (at the end). Irascible, "between" passions (hard-to-attain-lemonade) are hope and boldness.

Thomas, considering that *appetitus* entails both approach and avoidance, tells us that "the same, though opposite motions occur for repulsions." Consider dehydration as an evil other. The initiating, concupiscible passions in relation to dehydration would be hate and avoidance. Those are easy passions to have, considering the nature of the other. The irascible passions could be hope (to escape it), or fear (that you cannot), and anger (to resist it if it currently threatens you). Thomas cannot conceive that a self would ever be in complete union with an evil other; it would destroy the self. So he gives no concupiscible passion of union with an evil other. But if you could not at all avoid the evil of dehydration, you would have the irascible passion of sorrow. What is interesting is that even though the good or evil, the ease or difficulty, is *in the other*, it is *felt in the self* (as the passions of delight, for example, or fear with their attendant bodily changes). We can again see here how useful an interactive mode is for understanding Thomas' *Treatise on the Passions*.

Thomas considers good and evil to be in the other, and the self can con-form to that good or evil. A point of clarity is needed here. No creature can be evil in itself for Thomas, since, possessing being, it is good.[9] But a thing can be evil in a specific case, for a particular self (29.1ad1), or because there is so little good in the other, that it cannot help but cause difficulty (28.4ad2), usually because its being is primarily physical. We can never, after all our study, be tempted to say that Thomas considers the physical to be evil. It is, however, *limited* in that it cannot be widely shared, like that glass of lemonade, that only you can drink. Also, if it is primarily physical, it causes the self to engage it primarily on a physical level.[10] The self would then be in danger of dis-integrating the very organic (composite) nature which makes her to be what she is. She is in danger of becoming "alien to herself." On the other hand, the movement toward uniting with what is fitting for her as a rational being, is integrative—fulfilling.

In general, Thomas organizes the *Treatise on the Passions* around the two categories of concupiscible and irascible passions. He considers each concupiscible and irascible passion separately, and with each treatment gives us an increasingly rich understanding of the role of the passions in the formation of character. We will see highlights of his discussions later in this chapter. But now, you may have noticed that Thomas has a problem.

We are, as creatures, incomplete. We always need others to per-fect us. In the world, then, we are constantly being attracted to, or repulsed by, different object poles. We are in passion to all these oth-ers. Water, lemonade, iced tea attract us. Vegetables and meat and chocolates call to us. The conviviality of friends, neighbors, family inclines us toward them. The needs of abused and orphaned children in Jamaica can call us, as can the homeless in Appalachia. On the other hand, failure or poverty or violence can make us afraid. Injustice and suffering can make us angry. Aren't all these passions bad, then, rather than good? Confusing, distracting, perhaps paralyzing? Wouldn't it be better just to *think* our way through life, and not be distracted by the call of others, by all those passions? Can we hear Thomas' opponents marshaling their forces? What is Thomas going to say?

Thomas responds with a double thrust. He begins by quoting Augustine, who says that our passions will be bad if our love (*amor*) is bad, and good, if our love is good (24.1&2). In other words, it would seem right that we would need a single love which gives organization and form to all those attractions and repulsions. So, first, we need a paradigmatic relationship for which and through which all our other passions must be ordered. Second, Thomas says that the objects which cause our passions must be fitting[11] for a rational animal, who is made up of body, senses and spirit. Put those both together, and for Thomas the resolution is clear. He simply says that the most fitting, the most rational thing is to "love God, with all your strength, and all your heart, and all your mind," and that all our passions can be ordered by this passion for God.[12] Let us consider how Thomas accomplishes this.

III. The Self as Moved

First, let us look again at the rationality of a human being. Recall from Chapter 3 that rationality is the highest faculty in the human being. In the *Treatise*, Thomas uses rationality as the principle of organic unity for the whole human being. That allows him to say that passions are good inasmuch as they partake in rationality. "Just as it is better to both will the good and to act exteriorly to attain it, in the same way, it pertains to the perfection of moral (human) good not only to will the good, but actually to desire and delight in it with our corporeal desires and senses" (24.3). In the scientific studies of the first chapter, we have called that the "organic unity" of the human being. I believe that Descartes, and certainly Kant, would have found such a statement at least intriguing. We are more fully rational if we desire and delight in the good.

But rationality is the principle of interaction, too. The other, then, must be fitting for us in a rational way. Thomas says that what is fitting for the whole human being is something which "is received, as an object of passion, which is fitting for (*conveniens*), or in disharmony with (*dissonum*), the reason" (24.4). Thomas comes right out and says what is the most fitting other for the rationality of the human being. One might think, especially from reading our first chapter, that a human being's greatest aptitude is for other human beings, for their touch, without which we die. Thomas doesn't say that. He says that human beings' greatest aptitude (or hunger or thirst) is for God. "Therefore, love of a good which is fitting is a perfecting and improving of the one who loves. But love of a good which is not fitting[13] for the love is injurious and disintegrative. Thus a human being is most perfected and improved through the love of God" (28.5).[14]

That statement, of course, does not simply drop out of the sky. Thomas has prepared us for it throughout the *Summa*, as we have seen in Chapter 3. We also know that God and the angels share this intellective *appetitus* with humans (24.4ad2), and likes associate with likes in Thomas' theology. It is most interesting, however, to take that statement of God being fitting for the human being in the light of our most recent reflection on the composite nature (organic unity) of the human being. Thomas knows that we have bodies. He also knows that likes associate with likes, so he understands our fundamental needs for human touch and companionship. He also knows that God is pure Spirit. He has also read the *Nicomachean Ethics*, where Aristotle says that you would never want to have your friend become a god, because then the disparity of status would destroy the friendship. How can he say, then, that our most fitting other is God?

Thomas has, of course, a knowledge Aristotle never had, and could not have conceived of. His faith tells him that God has become a human being in the person of Jesus. So for him to know that we most need humanness, and to say that we most need God, is really for him to say the same thing. Even though Thomas does not explicitly mention the incarnation, he simply cannot be understood without it.

If we understand, then, that rationality is characteristic of the entire embodied organism, and that it "pertains to human good" to delight in the good physically as well as to reflect on it, the question of "How can I be fully 'rational?'" in the *Treatise on the Passions* can very well be put as: *How can I best be delighted?* And even though we have to skip ahead in the *Treatise* just a bit to see it, I believe we can already anticipate Thomas' answer. In Question 34.3, Thomas asks, "Is there any delight which is the best?" "Yes," Thomas says, and he quotes Psalm 16: "You will fill me with joy when I see Your face; in

Your right hand there will be pleasures forever more." "The greatest good and end for humans," Thomas says in the body of the article, "is God, who is simply the ultimate good (*summum bonum simpliciter*), whose enjoyment pertains to delight in the final goal."[15] It is that being delighted in our final goal, the communion of pure play[16] with God, that is, for Thomas, the most rational thing we can do. All our delights, all our passions must be aligned, must be caught up in the one great, most rational passion for God. That is, we must see that all the things which delight us, delight us because they are related to, partake in, the being and goodness of God.[17] To fasten on one of those relative delights as though it were absolute would be to be waylaid on our journey home to our "best delight." Thomas would say that if we choose a temporal good, like money, or status, or love of country as our highest good, we would be shortchanged in our quest for delight, and that is not rational at all. That is why in the very next question (34.4), Thomas can claim that pleasure is the standard by which we measure *all moral good and evil.* But perhaps we are getting ahead of ourselves. Let us be satisfied for now with a promise to return to Thomas' delightful discussion of the passion of delight.

Let us bring the body back into our discussion of rationality in the *Treatise*. Thomas says that the lower parts of the self can participate in rationality "by means of a 'resonating' (*per modum redundantiae*), in that the superior part of the soul (the rational *appetitus*) can be moved so intensely that the lower part of the soul follows its movement. In consequence there is activity in the sensate *appetitus* which is a sign[18] of the intention of the will" (24.4). That is, the entire organic unity—even in its physicality—literally becomes conformed to the object by which the intellective (rational) *appetitus* is being moved. I want to draw attention for a moment to Thomas' use of the word *redundantiae*, which I have translated as "resonating." There are several reasons for that translation. First, the Latin comes from the root word for "wave" (*undis*). Think of a plucked guitar string on a tuned guitar. Any plucked string will set up a sympathetic vibration (resonance) with the other strings; the same if you sing a note to which the guitar is attuned. If you consider all the strings of the guitar, all at once, you can see that they are all resonating (*redundantia*), sympathetically vibrating. That is what Thomas means here, and throughout the *Treatise*.[19] Contemporary scientific research, as we have seen, suggests a simultaneity in evaluation-perception, characteristic of the entire embodied organism.[20] That total simultaneous engagement of the whole self with the other is precisely what Thomas has in mind.

In keeping with our understanding of the organically unified engagement of the self with the other, we find passages in the *Treatise* where, conversely, bodily transmutations (changes) affect the intellective *appetitus* and the rational soul as well. And indeed a brief recollection reminds us that the very first article in the *Treatise* demonstrates Thomas' concern with attributing passions to the *soul*, because it is composite with the body. If we look specifically at 38.5ad3, we see that Thomas says explicitly that bodily dispositions (we called them "demeanors" in Chapter 1) can affect the soul. His objectors try to say that pain and sorrow cannot be relieved by baths and sleep. They say that such physical activity cannot change passions because they affect only the exterior senses and members (*exteriores sensus et membra*) and not the interior disposition of the heart (*interiorem cordis dispositionem*). Thomas, drawing on the organic unity of the human being, responds that "every good disposition of the body is in a kind of resonance (*redundat quodammodo*) with the heart, that is, with the source and end of bodily motion."[21] And there, Thomas has used the same *redundat*, to speak about how the body is also in harmony with—resonating with—the soul, so that something that affects the "outer person" can affect the "inner person" as well.[22] In short, the whole self is moving in concert. We see this understanding throughout the *Treatise on the Passions*. It opens Thomas to discussion with contemporary scientists, precisely on the issues of the knowing body, and the feeling mind.

In Chapter 1 we also spoke of the need to account for the self's virtually *instantaneous* evaluation of the other. We finally accepted an interactive model, where evaluation was not an isolated step, but a feature of the entire, embodied organism. It appears that Thomas makes the same observations about embodiment and instantaneous evaluation. In 1.77.7ad1, he writes, "Just as a power of the soul flows from it not by a process of change but by a natural resultance without sequence in time, so one power flows from another."[23] And in the *Treatise on the Passions,* he is presenting an interactive model of relationship between self and other, with the evaluation evident even in the basic bodily motions toward or away from the other. Again, Thomas' understanding very much resonates with the sense of current scientific studies, and with what we have been calling the interactive model.

We have focused on the other in Thomas' account of the passions. We then considered the self in passion, and began to see Thomas' understanding of their relationship as interactive. Good and evil, for example, is *in the other*, and *felt* in the *self*—in the whole, composite self. It is time now to make Thomas' own interactive model more clear. Thomas begins to make the interaction between self and other explicit in his discussion of the passion called love.

IV. The Interaction: The Body as Matrix

In 26.1, Thomas reviews the three kinds of *appetitus* with which we are already familiar (physical, sensate, and intellective), and their particular movements. In 26.2 ("Is love a passion?"), he says again that love is begun by the other, which acts as an agent. He refers us to "natural *appetitus*" as an example. "Something natural, when it is generating a physical reality, gives *weight* (*gravitatem*) to it, and the motion [that is proper to weight] follows along with that.[24] And it is the weight itself which is the principle of motion toward a place which is naturally fitting (*connaturalem*) for it on account of its weight." This is clear, and we have seen it before. The earth "generates" a stone. They share something in common, namely, weight. That very thing that they share (weight) causes the stone to move toward the earth when it is separated from the earth. In their sharing of weight, the earth and the stone are "co-natural" (*connaturalis*), and so belong together. After that example, Thomas goes on to apply this same principle to sensate and intellective *appetitus*. "In the same way, the thing which is desirable[25] gives to the desire-er a kind of 'fitting together with' for itself, which is a mutual pleasure of things desired. From that there follows motion toward what is desired."[26]

We can perceive a change as Thomas talks about the sensate and intellective *appetitus*, as subtle as a change of key in a Chopin nocturne. In natural *appetitus*, what is shared between two things, for example, is weight. The weight draws them together. What is shared on the higher levels, what draws them together, seems to be a kind of third thing: they share a common *pleasure*. Thomas has observed this.

When a stone gets to its "goal," the earth, it's there and that's it. But when dogs or humans achieve the goal of eating food, for example, they not only achieve their goal, but they can *take pleasure in it*. For Thomas it is significant that sensate and intellective creatures are drawn in a different way than stones. Animals and humans can *experience* passion. This is not only because they both have physical realities (rocks do), but because they both have a higher order of reason. Recall that, in Thomas' understanding, more reason means greater perception of beings, which means more delight.

Recalling Rorty's story of Ella and Louis in Chapter 2, we can ask Thomas how the relationship between two human beings can be rational, moral, and delightful. Thomas would respond that they can have mutual, or interactive desire for one another. But what is the nature of that desire? If you desire the other for himself, or for the way you feel when you are with him, that, according to Thomas, is just "con-cupiscentia." In our culture, we hear "concupiscent" sentiments sometimes expressed in songs, like "You Make Me Feel So Young." In the movie *Yentl*, Barbra Streisand sings, "I Love the Way He Makes Me Feel." Of course this is not an evil, but a good, since Thomas says, that "Whatever love there is has a certain participative similarity to divine love" (28.3). There is a "natural," mutual attractiveness that all humans have for each other. But the key to the morality of the relationship lies in threeness. If you and the other are drawn together because of a shared *good* in which you both take pleasure, that is the love called friendship (26.4).[27] In Thomas' schema, Ella and Louis must attend to the nature of the third, mutually shared good to determine the morality of their relationship.

Now we can see what Thomas intended when he "changed key" and described the higher forms of *appetitus* as the "mutual pleasure of shared desires." In the best, and most moral, relationships, Thomas believes, there are not two, but three. There is the self, the other, and the (mutually pleasurable) goods exchanged. Those goods exchanged determine the quality of the interaction; they are the medium of the relationship. The goods also determine the quality of the ones interacting. If only money is exchanged, then it is a business relationship. If all our relationships are business, then gradually, like Midas, we ourselves (and all we interact with) become conformed to money. If knowledge is exchanged, then it is better, since knowledge is shareable by many, and is more spiritual. If friendship is the highest form of the moral life, then our passions must conform to friendship if they themselves are to be moral.

From our study of the *Summa*, we can understand what is behind such a presentation of the importance of shared goods in the *Treatise on the Passions*. Thomas is thinking of the Trinity. The principle of unity, the good shared by Father and Son in their distinctiveness, is the Supreme Good: God—God the Holy Spirit. And it is that same Holy Spirit which God shares with us in the sacraments, that power that can and does draw us into fellowship with God, that makes us to be entirely who we are, and transforms us into other Christs, since God loves each one of us with the love of the first-born Child (cf. Heb 12:23). Spirit is the good that is exchanged between God and God's children, since "it is the Spirit which bears witness with our spirit that we are the children of God" (Rom 8:16). It is the distinctness of individuality, and the joy of intimacy in the Trinity (called "perichoresis") that underlies Thomas' ideas of fitting interaction in the passions. And it is the paradigmatic relationship of "friendship with God," the "best delight," which makes all our passions moral.

To sum up, it seems that the best way to understand what Thomas is saying about the morality of the passions is to use an interactive model, which attends to 1) the organic unity of the self, 2) interactions with the other, and 3) the interplay between organic unity and interactions with the other. And the good that will make all our relationships most moral is a shared passion for God.

Thomas himself is aware of those aspects of what we have called the interactive model. He refers to the interactive nature of the relationship when he writes that "the motion of the *appetitus* is *circular* [between the self and the other]."[28] Later in the *Treatise*, Thomas is much more explicit. He writes, "The motion of the *appetitus* part is from the inner part of the self, as though from the soul to the other. But the motion of the sensate part is from outside the self, as though from the other to the soul" (35.6ad2). Thus for Thomas, the other and the self are in interaction, moving toward each other, as it were.

And where do they meet? The body. That is why Thomas insisted on the centrality of the body from the beginning of the *Treatise on the Passions*. Thomas' technical way of describing what the body is doing in passion is to say that the bodily transmutations (changes) are the *material cause* of passions. We notice that they are not a result of passions, but one of the complex of *causes* of passion (cf. note 22). To use Thomas' own terms, union with the other is the *final cause* of all passions. Love is the *efficient cause* of the motion of the self toward the other. Love is also the *formal cause* of union between the self and the other. And the bodily changes are the *material cause* of the passions (28.5). The point is, again, that Thomas describes the bodily changes of passions as a feature of a total engagement of the self with the other. Thus, viewing the interaction from the point of view of the other, Thomas says that the bodily changes are materially caused by the other (28.5). From the other side of the interaction, the *appetitus* is ordered to (or away from) the object pole as it is in itself, and the bodily changes are the embodiment of the *appetitus* for (or away from) the object pole (cf. 22.2a3; 24.3a2; 31.4a2). Again, it seems best to consider relationship between other and self in Thomas as interactive, and, using the language of Chapter 1, to say that the body is the locus of interaction between the self and the other.

For Thomas, then, the body is not only that which individuates the self by setting the self off from other humans or objects. It is also essentially relational, the locus of the self's interaction with those who are other, since those others can cause their goodness or evil to be felt in harmony or disharmony with the self. Thus my body is the physical evidence both of my individuality and my vulnerability to (and need for) interrelationships.

This interactive model with its attention to the body holds even for Thomas' Christian understanding of the relationship between God and the human being. The human being seeks to return to God. God sees the inability of the human being to return because of sin, and God's love "moves" God to compassion. In compassion, God moves toward the human. Where do they meet? In the body—the body of Christ. Jesus then, always moved by compassion, "hit in his gut" by human suffering, is the embodiment of the love of God for human beings. Jesus is the meeting place for God and humans in the flesh. The model holds even when we reflect on the action of the Spirit from the perspective of the Trinity. The Spirit falls upon Mary, and the Word becomes flesh. The same Spirit falls upon us, and we become members of the body of Christ, the church. There, we meet God in the flesh.

Let us look further at how we are, in our embodiment, helped to integration by the other. All passion is movement (23.2). The movement toward full communion is in its own way delightful and more importantly *integrative* of the self. We are approaching what we are called (and empowered) to love, and in that approaching we are organizing, ordering, and integrating our powers in organic unity—concerting our intellect, will, and senses and physical movement toward achieving communion. Once we have attained that union, we have a richer kind of delight. But still, a certain kind of movement continues, because in that union the self is being continually *trans-formed* by communion with the other.[29] We can see how that description applies to the story of the worker and the lemonade. The lemonade calls to you, and you move toward it, integrating thought and will and senses and physical powers toward the goal of drinking it. The love and desire instilled in you to have that lemonade gives an admirable ordering and organizing (integration) of all your composite nature. You are moving, changing and, if you reflected about it, delighting in anticipation of drinking that lemonade. When you are drinking it, you have attained what you had a desire for, but you are still changing, as the lemonade quenches your thirst and restores you.

Throughout the *Treatise*, the bodily changes are an integral part of the human *appetitus*. All the activity of *appetitus* is in conformation with the other which is drawing it, with the goal of ultimately uniting with the other ("ad consequendas res"; see especially 37.4)—a union which also integrates the interior and exterior self. This attention to the body in love threatens to cause Thomas some difficulty in 28.5. His objectors have said that love is injurious to the lover, and one reason is that love causes "liquefaction." We are all familiar with this experience: getting "watery knees" when we see someone who sexually attracts us powerfully. Perhaps we have seen how a friend of ours "just melts" when he sees a baby. Does this not point to the dissolution of the organic unity of the self? And is this not injurious? No, says Thomas, because

> liquefaction is the opposite of hardening. That which is hardened is constricted into itself, and so has lost the capacity to permit the entrance of an other. It pertains to love, however, to achieve a certain permeability for the

goods of love, or for the presence of the beloved in the lover. So, a heart that is hard and tough is disposed to repudiate love. But liquefaction indicates a certain softening of the heart, which exhibits a readiness for the beloved to be welcomed in.

That is because

the lover is not content with a superficial knowing of the beloved, but strives to know from within, every single thing which pertains to the beloved, and so to enter into intimacy with the beloved. Thus we say about the Holy Spirit, which is the love of God, that it searches even the depths of God (27.2).

All love, with its attendant bodily changes, is for Thomas rooted in a passion for God.

In the *Treatise*, Thomas uses distinctive bodily changes to distinguish among passions, just as contemporary researchers do. We have seen, however, that Thomas is much richer in his account of these bodily changes. They not only distinguish between passions, they partake in the overall movement of the *appetitus* toward union with the other. Thus Thomas shows that "liquefaction" is not only characteristic of the total self moved by love, but also part of the self's readiness for union with the other. I find Thomas' account of embodied love and its purpose to be deeply insightful, but I am also struck by the sensitivity, for example, of his discussion of the body in sorrow or pain (*dolor*). In Question 38.2, Thomas asserts that sorrow or pain (*dolor*) is mitigated by weeping, "since everything sorrowful that is closed into the interior increases affliction, because more and more of the intent of the soul is absorbed by it. But when we pour it out into the body, then the 'cluster of intent' that the soul has invested in it, is likewise diffused into the exterior." This is a free translation, but it preserves Thomas' awareness of how preoccupying, afflicting and constricting sorrow is. More and more of the attention of our spirit is drawn to the sorrowful thing, if we "keep it in." The body, as it were, assists in restoring the balance to our intentionality, by drawing sorrow away and diffusing it in tears.

When Thomas discusses fear, he shows the same sensitivity both to the organic unity of the self, and its interaction with the other. The scholars are discussing whether or not fear causes contraction (44.1). Thomas' objectors have noticed that fear is characterized by a withdrawing of bodily heat and liquids to the interior of the person. But such an internal concentration would heat up the heart and internal organs, and so empower them to *attack*. Attacking is characteristic of those who are *angry*, not afraid. Thomas replies by reminding his objectors that bodily changes are the material cause of passions. Those changes are conformed to the other, such that the bodily changes correspond in similarity and rationality to the motion of the *appetitus*. Then he clarifies:

> In those who are fearful there is an internal contraction of vitality, but it is not the same as the contraction of those who are angered. In the latter the desire for vindication produces heat and a consequent thinning out of vital fluids …centered around the heart and mobilizing the person for attack. But in those who are frightened, an increasing frigidity results in the transfer of vital liquids from higher to lower regions, corresponding to the imagination of one's failing [falling] power. Heat and vital fluids are not concentrated around the heart, but flee from the heart. That is why those who are afraid do not go forward quickly, but flee (ad2).

Thomas acknowledges some similarity between anger and fear, but his attention to the subtle differences allows him to distinguish the two. We saw the same method of distinction between fear and anger among contemporary scientific researchers. The coldness of fear (as opposed to the heat of anger) has impressed Thomas. We say, "he was frozen with fear," "she went cold with fear," or even, "it was fearfully (not angrily) cold." But Thomas insists that those bodily changes have a purpose in their relationship to the other. In that, Thomas would agree with Darwin that those bodily changes are organizing, preparing the self for a "fitting interaction" with the other: fight (anger) or flight (fear) or perhaps "freezing" (maybe he won't see me).

To sum up our reflections on the body in these last paragraphs, we can use the language of Chapter 1. In interaction with the other,

Thomas sees the bodily transmutations (changes) as *incipient purposive actions* ordered toward approach or avoidance of the other. As such, they are features of the total organism's engagement with the other. Those bodily changes are purposive precisely because they are composite with (organically unified with) rationality in the human being, and, as such, participate in the entire organism's evaluation of the other. But we call them incipient, because they are not yet finalized; they need to complete their movement, whose final goal is communion with the other. Thomas likens those bodily changes to "snap judgments" in 45.4, in his discussion of boldness. The body, he says, is making decisions, but they are snap decisions. Recall Pribram's monkeys, making the decision to push the button *before* the signals reach the visual cortex. In order to get those snap decisions to partake in "long range planning,"[30] to be deliberative and comparative, we need rationality, since deliberation and comparison are characteristic of rationality. We need to integrate the energy of the passions, and the vision of the reason. We need to have our passions be fully rational, and a fully rational passion would be a virtue.

Everything we have discussed about the body in passion applies, and paradigmatically, to the passion for God in the self. It fits the overall sense in the *Summa* of the creature being called to communion with God. God creates the human being in God's own image and likeness. And instilling that likeness in the human being has initiated a call to— a passion for—communion with God's own self. That communion with God is the final goal, and best delight. As the self moves closer and closer to God, the self becomes more and more delighted, more and more integrated, more and more itself, and so more and more like God.

We said in the beginning of this chapter that Thomas' insistence on the importance of the body in passion would even allow him to tell us how to be holy, as God is holy. He has a systematic and logical way to make the sanctification of the body explicit in the *Treatise on the Passions.* In Question 30.1, on concupiscence, Thomas is insisting on the organic unity (composite nature) of the self in passion. He understands that the senses of themselves cannot sense God, because they are physical. On the other hand, he says, the body *is* a part of an organic unity. Thus the love of spiritual things can be called *con-cupiscence* because "spiritual love has a certain similarity to sensate love." That desire for spiritual things is also called *con-cupiscence* because of

> the intensity of the *appetitus* of the superior part [of the composite for spiritual things]. From that there is a resonance in the lower *appetitus* [the sensate and physical] so that simultaneously the lower *appetitus* in its own way moves toward spiritual good, following together with the higher *appetitus*, with the result that *even the body itself is deserving of spiritual things*—just as it says in the Psalms, "My heart *and my flesh* rejoice in the living God" (ad1).

That, then, is Thomas' systematic and logical way of speaking about the divinization of the embodied human being, and I believe he is speaking about meditation (cf. 38.4a3). He fully expects that answering Christ's call to pray always will transform and sanctify the body in a passion for God. In fact, later in the *Treatise*, when Thomas discusses whether pain or sorrow (*dolor*) is mitigated by contemplation of the truth, Thomas again refers to the sanctification of the body in his affirmative reply:

> We have seen that the contemplation of truth is the greatest of all delights. We have also seen that every delight mitigates pain; and it does so the more, the more perfectly one loves wisdom. That is why people find joy in the midst of tribulation by contemplating the things of God and the happiness to come, as the Epistle of James says, "Consider yourselves happy indeed, my sisters and brothers, when you encounter trials of every sort" (1:12). What is more, this joy occurs even in the midst of bodily torture. Thus the martyr Tiburtius, walking barefoot on burning coals, said, "I feel that I am walking on roses, in the name of Jesus Christ" (38.4).

It may seem foolish to us that such an intellectual as Thomas believes that story of Tiburtius. But if we reflect, we see that Thomas is not only piously, but intellectually committed to the transformation of the entire self, such that even the body shares in spiritual delights.

He believes that the passion for God can so suffuse the entire self that we ourselves become, as it were, sacraments of the living God. "And all of us," writes Paul, "with our unveiled faces like mirrors reflecting the glory of the Lord are being transformed into the image that we reflect in brighter and brighter glory; this is the working of the Lord who is the Spirit" (2 Cor 3:18).

V. Rational, Moral Passions

We need to summarize and clarify Thomas' understanding of how a person is to be morally responsible for how she *feels*, for her passions. How are we to have the passions in the right way, at the right time, to the right extent, toward the right person? Thomas' answer to that is very simple, but his account of it is very rich, as we have seen all through our discussion of the *Treatise*. Thomas would simply say that all our passions must be rational. We must have passions as a rational animal would have them—one who "combines, as it were, the eternal and temporal in one horizon" (G.G. II 81). Let us look specifically at what Thomas says about rationality in the *Treatise on the Passions.*

Early in the *Treatise*, Thomas says that we can think of passions morally not when we consider them "in and of themselves" (*secundum se*) but only inasmuch as they are "placed under (*subjacent*) the governance (*imperio*) of reason and will." Now there is a powerful temptation to the modern reader, assisted by Descartes and popular culture, to read that statement as saying: (a) passions (emotions) "in themselves" are morally neutral;[31] (b) passions then "acquire" morality by being "subjected"[32] to reason, or will.[33] That simply cannot be.

When we take such a statement in the context of the whole *Treatise on the Passions,* and even of the whole *Summa*, we see why such an understanding of "control" of the passions by reason does not fit. First we recall Thomas' insistence on the organic unity of the "composite" being; it would be a violation now to present passions as a separate parcel in human operations. Further, this is the only time in the *Treatise on the Passions* that Thomas speaks of the passions in this way, and twice he uses the verb "to be considered" (*considerari*), meaning that he is only thinking this way for the sake of a discussion.[34]

But when Thomas discusses human passions, he says that they are *already* (by virtue of creation) ordered to reason.[35] Of course, in another sense they are *not yet* fully governed by reason, since then we would be in union with God.[36] The morality of the passions refers to a process of finalizing or completing or fully integrating passions that are already disposed toward rationality by virtue of their participation in a composite, rational being. That process is hardly captured by the phrase, "submitting passions to rational control."[37]

We find an even deeper problem if we think that Thomas means for us to submit our passions to control by the reason. The problem is that reason (understood as mental, or contemplative activity) cannot get us to our final goal of union with God as well as our passions can. We have already seen from our study of the *Summa* that love and not the intellect is our best way of approaching God. We expect to hear Thomas say the same thing here in the *Treatise on the Passions*, and he does. In 27.2ad2, Thomas writes,

> That which is required for the perfection of knowledge is not required for the perfection of love.... Love is in the *appetitus* power, which regards a thing as it is in itself, so that for the perfection of love it suffices that a thing is loved as it is perceived in itself... and the same holds true for the love of God.

That is because "a human being is able to move toward God through a 'passive love,' inasmuch as she *is attracted* by God's own self, more so than her intellect can lead her to God, since [the former] pertains to the characteristic of delight" (24.4ad4).

Those who wish to adduce Thomas in support of cognitivism, or claim that he is "excessively intellective," might benefit from study of those two questions.[38] But it is also consoling to see what Thomas' systematic commitment to passion can do for us. I, along with so many others, suffered with a parent who was a victim of Alzheimer's disease. If we understand Thomas correctly here, we see that God did not stop calling her to God's self because she could no longer understand what was happening to her, or actively cooperate in that call. She needed only to "move toward God through a passive love" as God was revealing God's self to her. In the end she lost all rational and voluntary movement, and was only a physical presence. But even then, inasmuch as she was subject to *gravity,* God was still present to her, drawing her in her "natural *appetitus,*" and so attracting her whole self, since she is a composite, as Thomas would say. And in that extreme, we can see a broader truth in the *Summa* and the *Treatise on the Passions:* holiness does not consist in understanding, but in having the self be totally drawn by the love of God's own self, in whatever way God chooses to move the self. Holiness consists in a passion for God.

Thomas himself gives us the best way for understanding how to have moral, rational passions, when he says in the last passage quoted that the final goal pertains to *delight.* Earlier in this chapter, we had seen how "what is most rational" is equivalent to "what is most delightful." Let us study how Thomas uses the passion of delight to illumine what he means by rationality.

Thomas says that "delight in the affections of the soul is proportionate to *quies* in natural (physical) bodies" (31.8; cf. 23.4). Thomas' two terms, delight (*delectatio*) and *quies* (broadly, "rest"), illumine each other. On the level of natural *appetitus,* when a stone is taken away from the earth, then released, it returns to its natural place, and has *quies* (rest) there. But on the level of sensate *appetitus* (animals), something different happens. An animal can pursue what it wants, because, having a soul, it has freedom in a way that a rock does not. Further, as we have seen, its higher rational power enables it to experience *delight.*[39] When the animal attains its goal (when it meets its caretaker, or is eating its food), the animal has a *quies* different from the stone. The animal has its *quies,* but *with cognition* (27.3). What is characteristically *cognitional* about the passions of animals is that an animal can *delight* in reaching its goal (food, caretaker) (31.5; cf. 41.3). A stone cannot.

Thomas has told us how the passion of delight distinguishes physical from sensate *appetitus.* Now, to account for the third level of *appetitus,* Thomas must tell us what it means to have a *rational* delight.[40] How does the delight of a rational animal differ from the delight of an animal? First, in a human being, reason "governs" delight by making sure that the delight does not go beyond certain bounds. That would be irrational, not because a passion has escaped "rational control," but because, beyond certain bounds, *pleasure ceases to be pleasure,* and that is undesirable.[41] In one way, Thomas is simply reminding us of what we all know. "I should not have drunk so much!" "I wish I had stopped before I had that extra piece of pie." But what is important is Thomas' claim that this is one test for whether your passions are rational, and so, *moral:* Are you consistently delighted?

And again, why is delight so important for a *rational* creature who can see his final goal? Thomas tells us that "delight" is related to "dilate," that is, "expansion" (cf. 33.3 and 4). There is a popular play called *Your Arms Too Short to Box with God.* What Thomas says is: our hearts are too narrow, too constricted, too closed to delight in the Ultimate Delight. So we must be trained on our way back to God, trained by the various "delights" that God gives us, until our hearts are "dilated" enough, expansive enough, to embrace God.

All the delights of our world, then, are not just delightful in themselves. They have a purpose. They are part, too, of the great return of creation to its home, and to be rational, to be moral, we must see them, *and our interaction with them*, in the light of that purpose which we share with them.[42] Their goodness draws us, and our rationality guides them, in return to God. That is another way that God has of "sharing goods" with us. As intellective creatures, we can see, delight in, and cooperate with God's purpose for creation in a way that animals cannot. God shares God's vision for creation with us, and we can together share the "mutuality of shared desires." To sum up, each good shares in the One Good. Therefore each good for which we have a passion draws us in our organic unity closer to the Ultimate Good. This one, paradigmatic relationship affects and draws us through all the goods in the world. Those goods are in a way like relay posts, passing us on to God.

For Thomas, it is completely rational to love God, with all your heart, and all your soul, and all your strength, since that, as we have seen, is the greatest delight. And surely it would be foolish to mistake a temporal delight, perceived only by the senses, for that eternal delight, which satisfies *both* the "heart and the flesh" forever. What do we do, then, with all the particular, temporal delights? How are we to have them train us for the ultimate delight? Thomas would say this. In our sensate *appetitus*, we can delight in sensate, temporary things, like chocolate, sunsets, having and raising children, flowers, learning. In our intellective *appetitus*, we can anticipate with delight our final end: eternal joy with God.[43] The most rational act for composite beings, who can delight in the particular and the eternal, is to fuse both those powers, and to *see the eternal in every particular,* to appreciate the presence of God to every being, or, to put it in Ignatius' terms, to find God in all things. Our movement toward God, then, integrates our higher and lower desires, such that we can, literally, physically *"hunger and thirst* for justice"—and be satisfied.

Thomas has a clear and concise way of putting all that, of course. It has to do with the *quies* of a rational being. The *quies* of an animal was characterized by "cognition," which gave it *delight.* What is characteristic of the rational being? Not only that she "recognizes" that she has attained her goal, but that she can *reflect* on it. Human beings can finalize their approach or avoidance, take delight in that finalization, and then, distinctively, *deliberate on the passion of delight.* And when the human being reflects, as a human being, on her delight, the *quies* changes. It is more properly called "pure play." The delight changes. It becomes *joy.* I had a friend who described once the delight of biting into a freshly picked, vine-grown tomato. When, *from within that delight,* she reflects on the generosity of God, on God's giving her the ability to delight in this tomato, on God's nurturance of the whole world, she experiences *joy.* She has found the *meaning* of her delight. And that, for Thomas, would be rational, human, moral passion. Joy is the consummate passion of the moral life. And it remains a passion because it is in interaction with our final goal, whose love attracts us through all the delights and joys of our lives. More simply put, to make your passions fully moral, have all your delights be joy. In that, we hear Thomas' echo of Paul's moral commandment to the Philippians, "Rejoice in the Lord always. Again I say it: rejoice!" (4:4).

In the last part of the *Treatise on the Passions,* Thomas traces a similar pattern of "making passions fully rational" in his discussions of the various "irascible" passions (those which we have for a good which is difficult to attain, or an evil which is hard to avoid), such as boldness or anger, pain or sorrow. In those discussions Thomas is more careful, because "delight perfects an operation," but sorrow or pain (*dolor*) inhibits the natural motion which is the essence of human life.[44] In the realm of "irascible" passions, pain (*dolor*) is parallel to delight (*delectatio*), and sadness (*tristitia*) is parallel to joy (*gaudium*).[45]

What good is there, then, in a passion such as sorrow, for example? It is not "natural" for us to be sorrowful, says Thomas, since it prevents the *quies* (pure play) of the rational *appetitus*. But we need it to move us away from just the things that would take away our joy. If it is evil to delight in evil things, then it is *morally good if we are sad about evil.*[46]

The same is true for shame (*turpis*), for example. If we *judge* that something shameful has been done (this is possible solely for rational beings), then it is morally good to be ashamed. And suppose we find that a child has been abused. Then it is good to be sad about it, and not to move toward putting it right would be a "manifest evil" (39.1), since that move in opposition to evil is one purpose of an irascible passion. But suppose we cannot, for whatever reason, overthrow an evil. Then, says Thomas, a morally good person would "bear with it, and groan" (28.4).

In the end, we see that the passions are crucial in the moral life, since what affects you reveals your moral character, reveals who you are. To paraphrase the old scholastic adage, "*Passio* sequitur esse." A person's moral character is displayed by what causes him delight or pain, by what moves him, by his passions.

We need to make a few more observations about the *Treatise on the Passions* before we leave it. After the *Treatise*, Thomas turns to the discussion of dispositions and habits. Actually, we find threads of that discussion throughout the *Treatise* as well. For example, in the interaction between the subject pole and object pole, Thomas says that the form of the object pole creates a *habit* of *appetitus* toward itself in the subject pole. The *material* of that habit is the bodily changes (28.5). In other words, the self in passion is *physically habituated* to the other. We have already seen this in our scientific studies in Chapter 1. We used it to explain why it took so long to change passions, even after our evaluations had changed. Passions endure, we said, because they have become embodied—we have grown physically habituated to the other. That is, the body as a spatio-temporal reality lends historicity to passions, since, as Thomas says, "When bodily matter receives forms, it holds those forms not only during the time when those forms are acting upon it, but even after those forms have ceased to perform their action" (I.79.6). Thus historicity, one of the features of *habit*, is characteristic of passions precisely in their *embodiment*. That is why the *Treatise on the Passions* can be considered to be the crucial beginning point for an ethic of Christian virtue—an ethic of sanctification, especially sanctification of the body, since the best passion for human beings is a passion for God, so that "my heart and my flesh rejoice in the living God."

In the *Treatise on the Passions*, we have seen that passions need to be integrated with rationality in order for us to have the passions "in the right way, at the right time, to the right extent, etc." The integration of reason and passion allows us to turn "snap decisions" to "long range planning." We also need rationality, then, for our passions to endure—for the right passions to become *habitual* for us. Just such an habitualized right passion would, it seems to me, be a *virtue*. That would explain why Thomas places the *Treatise on the Passions* here, before his discussion of habit, which in turn is before his discussion of virtue. It also in part explains Thomas' emphasis on the *body* in the *Treatise*.

I believe, though, that Thomas has another reason for spending so much time here on the passions. Especially in the *Treatise on the Passions*, Thomas presents habits as interrelational. He takes seriously the fact that we are created by God, that we need God, and that we come toward God better through being drawn, being loved, *being moved,* than by our own direct efforts. The passions, then, can be understood as receiving an empowerment from an other. Whether from food, or conversation, or prayer, we are always being, in our different dimensions, "energized" by the other. It would be rational and virtuous, then, to organize this energizing, so that it fulfills us as a rational being, *and* empowers us to move toward our final goal. When sunlight falls upon a rock, for example, it energizes it by heating it. When the same sunshine falls upon a leaf, it energizes it not only by heating it, but by nourishing it. That is because the leaf has chlorophyll, which both makes it to be a leaf, and enables a more thoroughgoing interaction with the sunshine by photosynthesis. On this analogy, we can liken the sunshine to the other, and the chlorophyll to virtue. Human virtue would "translate" passivity into activity. Thomas needs this discussion of virtue, then, because it is not only the province of virtue that we *act* in the right way. It is the province of virtue—and especially important for Thomas' theology—that we *are moved* in the right way, at the right time, to the right extent. That we are, first of all, moved by a passion for God.

For Thomas, then, the human being is a "moved mover." Therefore, when he considers both features of human moral responsibility, he presents us with two interrelated understandings of moral agency. We first see this stated in I-II.3.2.ad3, in Thomas' discussion of the perfection of the human being by happiness. "There are two sorts of operation. One goes out from the agent and works on the material which is external to her, e.g., burning, cutting, etc. The other remains within the agent, e.g., feeling, thinking, willing—and this sort is a perfection of the agent herself." We have seen that distinction before, in Chapter 2. We call the first kind of operation (action) *transitive agency*. We call the second kind of operation (passion) *immanent* [remaining within] *agency*. Aquinas holds that happiness is an operation in the second sense. He takes up the same theme in the *Treatise* in the discussion of delight (31.1ad2). For Thomas, then, the perfection of the agent lies in passion. Happiness, or, better, the passion of joy, is the perfection of the agent; it is caused by the other, and remains in the self. The problem, as we have seen, with so many accounts of agent-responsibility is that they try to talk about the perfection of the agent, but say that the agent is only responsible for his (transitive) *actions*. Throughout the *Treatise*, Thomas is speaking about *immanent* agency. In his discussion of "rational passions," he is showing us how to speak about agent-responsibility for the *passions*. Because the other through love causes passions, Thomas' account is open to that broader notion of agency that we postulated as necessary in Chapter 2: that of being an "agent *for*," acting on behalf of, an other. And for Thomas, of course, we are all supposed to be agents of God.

If we say, then, that somehow we are responsible for our passions, that responsibility must also be principally receptive. It would have more to do with acceptance than activity, more to do with gratitude than productivity.[47] Put another way, we are responsible for how we take things—for the *meaning* that things have for us. Meaning, as we have seen, is crucial for passions, because it lies at the "intersection of cognition and affect."

Thomas is aware of the importance of meaning in passions, of how we take things, and he sometimes discusses that feature of passions under the rubric of *imagination*. Thomas sees imagination primarily as a faculty of the senses, which integrates immediate sense knowledge with the internal faculty of memory in creative ways. Thomas points out that the imagination deeply affects our passions. He speaks, for example, about why it is easier to walk a plank close to the ground rather than the same plank over a chasm (44.4ad2). He says that this is due to a disturbance in the imagination, which causes the fear: we have taken the plank differently. Thomas also says that our sensate passions for higher goods (such as a hunger and thirst for justice) occurs through the medium of imagination (30.3ad3). That surely is how the self can take responsibility in the interaction with the other, by attending to the imagination, to how the self takes things. Thomas, however, is not strong in his discussion of the imagination in the *Treatise on the Passions.* We will have to wait for Ignatius to tell us better how to change our imagination of others, and how to hunger and thirst for the reign of God.

We should close this chapter by reflecting again on the story of Fabian from the perspective of the *Treatise on the Passions.* Thomas says that for us not to move against an evil would indicate that we do not have the right passion, which in turn indicates we do not have the right dispositions.[48] There is something morally very wrong, Thomas would say, if we are not angry with war, enraged with rape, bold in siding with the oppressed, zealous in our defense of the poor, moved with compassion for an abused child. That is why God gave us those *interactive* passions. When Fabian's little brother first drew back from him in fear, it was *fitting* and morally right for Fabian to be distressed. He came to his community to find the *meaning* of the action, the right reason for it. Then, Thomas would say, he could govern the power of his irascible passions to move toward the "concupiscible" passion: delight in shared touch, shared projects, and shared play. And something more. All through their struggle, the community of "big brothers" kept supporting each other, praying together, and reading scripture together. Our hope was in God. Thomas says that hope is the irascible passion that deals with "possible to be in union with," and that it is possible to be in hope by the helping power of another (40.2). So, as old habituations died, and new, fulfilling relationships took their place, we could, in our delight, be grateful to the One in the hope of whose love all this was accomplished. Years later, Fabian wrote me a letter in which he said, "I am so glad that I know for myself what the gospel means." I am grateful for that, that we shared in the good of the gospel. I believe, too, that Fabian would smile at Thomas' account of the passions, and understand him when he speaks of joy.

5.

A PASSION FOR GOD:
THE SPIRITUAL EXERCISES
OF IGNATIUS OF LOYOLA

All I want is to know Christ and the power of his resurrection and to share his sufferings by reproducing the pattern of his death.

—St. Paul, *To the Philippians*

In this chapter we will reflect on two interrelated works of Ignatius of Loyola: his *Autobiography* and his *Spiritual Exercises*. In the *Exercises* we will find a practical way of working out in prayer the topic of this book: a passion for God. In the *Autobiography*, Ignatius presents us with his own story as an example of what a life led in a passion for God might look like, or, more properly, feel like.

I. An Overview: Ignatius of Loyola and His *Spiritual Exercises*

Iñigo Lopez de Loyola was the youngest of thirteen children born in 1491 to a noble Basque family in the old kingdom of Castille. At the beginning of a long war between Spain and France, Iñigo found himself in charge of the Spanish garrison in the citadel of the Pamplona, holding out against the French who had already conquered the rest of the city. Though his men urged surrender, Iñigo insisted on continuing the resistance. In the subsequent bombardment, a cannonball shattered his leg, and the garrison quickly surrendered. His *Autobiography* begins at that point, on May 20, 1521.[1]

In the *Autobiography*, Ignatius (he took that name some ten years later, during his studies in Paris, probably out of admiration for Ignatius of Antioch) recounts several nearly fatal operations to repair his shattered leg. (They never fully succeeded, and he was left with a permanent limp.) His description of one of those operations gives us a good insight into the truly "machismo" character of this young Basque, and his attitude toward the passions. The crudeness of a previous operation left him with a piece of shin bone growing out of his leg. Thinking of the tight, form-fitting hose fashionable in his day, the young Iñigo told his doctors to saw it off. They said that they would, but that "the pain would be greater than all those that he had suffered, because it was already healed and it would take some time to cut it …but the wounded man [Iñigo] endured it with his customary patience." And what was that "customary patience"? Ignatius tells us: "he never uttered a word nor showed any sign of pain other than to clench his fists" (22). Descartes, I believe, would have been proud.

Before, however, we dismiss Ignatian spirituality as having little to tell us about the passions, other than to "be strong," as our prevailing popular model tells us, we need to examine Iñigo's story just a bit more. The story of the operation was a pre-conversion story. Ignatius' strength would find a different expression, and a much different picture is presented to us later in the *Autobiography*. One day, in the course of his prayer, "the pilgrim" (as Ignatius calls himself throughout the *Autobiography*), received a profound insight into the Trinity. He tells us that this insight

> brought on so many tears and so much sobbing that he could not control himself. While going in a procession that set out from there that morning, he could not hold back his tears until dinnertime; after eating he could not stop talking about the Most Holy Trinity, using many different comparisons and with great joy and consolation (38).

Ignatius went from being a man who clenched his fists to one who poured out his tears all day long, from one who never uttered a word to one who could not stop talking, so great was his joy and consolation.

What happened? Between those two events, Ignatius experienced a *conversion* to God. What is most interesting for this book, of course, is how that conversion changed his vision, and so his *passions.*

In the course of convalescence from his injury, Ignatius discovered that thoughts of doing great things for God gave him longer-lasting happiness than his dreams of a life of chivalry. So he determined to leave his castle at Loyola and become a pilgrim to the holy land. But on the way he stopped at the town of Manresa, where he spent about ten months fasting, praying, visiting the sick, taking counsel from spiritual persons, and in general engaging in "spiritual exercises." When he had completed this schooling, he began to write down what he had learned, so that he might help others to come to the conversion and vision which so consoled and strengthened him. Beginning then, and throughout the rest of his life, he would add to and edit those "notes," have them challenged by the Inquisition, and eventually present them as his *Spiritual Exercises.*[2]

It is as hard to understand those *Exercises* from reading the text as it is to get the flavor of a baseball game by reading the rule book. That is because "the book of the *exercises* is not a theological work attempting to present a Christology but a practical work fostering an encounter with Christ."[3] The book of the *Exercises* has instructions for both retreatant and director for a retreat of thirty days, divided into four "Weeks" of varying length. "The *first part* is devoted to the consideration and contemplation of sin; the *second part* is taken up with the life of Christ our Lord up to Palm Sunday inclusive; the *third part* treats of the passion of Christ our Lord; the *fourth part* deals with the Resurrection and Ascension..." (*SE*, 4). The retreatant spends four to five hours in meditation each day, and sees his director usually once each day. In addition, the retreatant is instructed, after each meditation, to reflect upon the movements which occurred during the meditation (as Ignatius did during his convalescence) and to examine his conscience twice each day. Often eucharist is celebrated daily. The *Exercises* also instruct the director in the kinds of prayer, fasting and penances which might be appropriate at different times in the retreatant's ongoing encounter with the Lord.

In this chapter, I want to consider that the purpose of the *Exercises* is to *train the passions,* so that the retreatant's passions can be transformed, much as Ignatius' own passions were transformed and inflamed with the love of God and the service of God's reign. As we study the *Exercises,* we will see that Ignatius' understanding of the passions is quite close to that of Thomas, and quite congenial to the contemporary interactive model of the passions.

In the *Exercises,* Ignatius is most concerned with being moved, with the passions. In fact, in one of the earliest instructions to the director of the *Exercises,* Ignatius insists that being moved is essential to the dynamics of the retreat. He says that if the director perceives that "no spiritual movements are coming to the one who is making the *Exercises,* such as consolations or desolations, that she is not stirred by different spirits," then the director ought to check carefully, because the retreatant is not doing the exercises properly (6). The whole of the *Exercises* is concerned with being moved by God toward God. Ignatius expects the retreatant to *experience* what Thomas presented in his theology. That is, as the retreatant moves closer to God, she should feel increasing peace (*quies*),[4] delight and joy, which Ignatius calls *consolation.* On the other hand, the retreatant can tell when she is being drawn away from her fitting interaction with God, since she will experience increasing turmoil, disquiet and unhappiness, which Ignatius calls *desolation.* We will hear Ignatius draw our attention to those passions throughout the spiritual journey that is the *Exercises.* He expects such passions, properly trained by the *Exercises,* to guide us reliably all through our life's journey back to God our home.

In particular, Ignatius requires the retreatant to begin every meditation by asking God explicitly for *what she desires* in that exercise (48), and often suggests that the retreatant should ask to feel "the right way." And for Ignatius, to be moved in the right way is to be moved as Jesus was moved. And how is that accomplished? We are to accompany Jesus through all the journey of his life, and his life's mission of justice, compassion and liberation. Ignatius knows that during that journey we will be drawn by God into a profound relationship with Jesus, will become attuned to him, will come to exchange confidences and goods as friends do. He knows that we will be forever moved by the God whose love moved him from heaven to the passion, and from the cross to glory. From then on, each sorrow—from the loss of a parent to the loss of a virtue—will find in him consolation and redemption. Each delight—from a sunset to a wedding—will lead us back to him "in whose light we see light." And all our passions—from a passion for chocolate to a passion for justice—will be caught up in the love of the "One who loved me and gave himself up for me." In short, we will come to feel as Jesus feels, because we will be in Love with him.

If we take the *Exercises* as a training in passion, then, it is easy to understand why, in his directions to the very first meditation in the *Exercises*, Ignatius writes, "[I]n a contemplation on the Resurrection I will ask for joy *with Christ in joy*. In one on the Passion [of Our Lord], I will ask for sorrow, tears, and anguish *with Christ in anguish*" (Puhl, 48, emphasis added). Ignatius presents Jesus as Aristotle's expert, teaching us how to be moved in the right way. Let us turn to the *Exercises* to see the pattern of that transformative journey with Christ.

II. The First Week: "I Once Was Lost, But Now Am Found...."

Ignatius begins the *Exercises* with the "Principle and Foundation" (23). God has made us for himself, Ignatius tells us, and finding God will preserve the self.[5] Further, all created things with which we are in interaction must be seen in light of our final goal. We should choose whatever brings us closer to God and free ourselves of whatever holds us back—like Thomas' rock, falling freely and naturally back to its rest when it is no longer impeded. Even things which seem to happen to us—like health or sickness, wealth or poverty, long or short life—should have meaning for us only insofar as they help us in our return to God. The first official Jesuit commentary on the *Exercises* calls this introduction "the basis of the whole moral and spiritual edifice" (*Dir.*, Ch. 12, 1). From our perspective, we might see it as a succinct summary of Thomas' *Treatise on the Passions*.

The retreatant first meets Jesus in the first meditation of the First Week—but not right away. Ignatius first wants her to experience what it feels like to be separated from God. This first meditation is a meditation on sin and on hell, and Ignatius wants the retreatant to ask for the passions of "shame and confusion" (*SE*, 48). Ignatius believes, with Aquinas, that it is *natural* for human beings (and for all creation) to be with God. All sorrow, then, all shame and confusion comes from a rupture in this natural relationship (*SE*, 10).[6] Ignatius asks the retreatant to contemplate the sin of the angels,[7] then the sin of Adam and Eve, then the enormity of a single mortal sin against God. The sense that Ignatius wants the retreatant to get from this first meditation is that sin has a history and a reality apart from the retreatant. From that perspective she can see sin as a reality that besets her, attacks her, victimizes her. She gradually realizes that she herself has become slave to those abusive dynamics and worse—a collaborator who in turn harms herself and others. But then, at the most desperate moment, Ignatius introduces the retreatant to Christ—and him crucified:

> Imagining Christ our Lord before you and present on the cross, begin a dialogue with him: how is it that the Creator has come to be a human being, and come from eternal life to take up death in time, and thus come to die for my sins? (53).

That is Ignatius' intention in the meditation on sin: not to get the retreatant to feel guilty, but to establish a dialogue with Jesus who liberates and saves her. One is reminded of Paul, whose letter had caused distress for the Corinthians, writing "I wrote to you…not meaning to cause you distress, but to show you how much I love you" (2 Cor 2:4).

When, in the second meditation of the First Week, Ignatius asks the retreatant to reflect on his own personal sins and their consequences, again he seeks not to instill guilt, but to overcome it. Thus the final point of the meditation is not a groan of shame but a "cry of wonder" (*SE*, 60), not an abject humiliation but a grateful dialogue in which the retreatant "extols the mercy of God our Lord…giving thanks to Him that up to this very moment He has granted me life" (61). We notice that Ignatius' understanding of sin is surely different than that of our popular culture. In popular culture, for example, we might hear a certain dessert advertised as "it's so good, it's 'sinful.'" The understanding of sin seems to be that sin is something fun that we really shouldn't do. What would a savior look like in that context? Someone who tries to convince us that having fun is bad.

But with Ignatius, the retreatant understands sin as what it is—a besetting reality that deforms, demeans and disfigures him. Once, several members of my upper division class reported that a group of young men outside their door screamed racist remarks at them. I invited the class to imagine the faces of those young men, twisted as they must have been in hatred. I then asked them to see that misshapenness as a physical mark reflecting the action of sin upon a person. If the retreatant understands sin correctly, then he can look to Jesus with gratitude and joy; here is his savior, his liberator who frees him from the deformity of sin. We are reminded of Paul's words, then: "Wretch that I am, who shall redeem me from this body doomed to die? Praise be to God through our Lord Jesus Christ!" (Rom 7:24-25).

There are two interesting features of these early meditations: the dialogue (which Ignatius calls the "colloquy"), and the use of the imagination. Since Ignatius employs them throughout the *Exercises*, we should examine them now.

Ignatius immediately annotates the dialogue (colloquy) of the first meditation by saying:

> The colloquy is made by speaking exactly as one friend speaks to another, or as a servant speaks to a master, now asking him for a favor, now blaming himself for some misdeed, now making known his affairs to him, and seeking advice in them (*SE*, Puhl, 54).

The words of the popular hymn "In the Garden" say, "He walks with me and He talks with me." That is precisely the experience that Ignatius wants the retreatant to have, beginning here at the start of the *Exercises,* and continuing throughout his life. Again, Ignatius' point is a practical application of Thomas' insights. Thomas defined charity as "friendship with God" (I-II.65.5). Thomas also sees charity as "the form of all the virtues." In his logic, then, friendship with God is the form of all the virtues. When Ignatius concludes every meditation in the *Exercises* by dialoguing with Jesus "exactly as one friend speaks to another," he is urging the retreatant continually to understand all her passions as features of this dialogue, this interactive relationship, this friendship with God.

The principal means Ignatius uses for turning our passions into a passion for God throughout the *Exercises* is by employing the *imagination.* He is constantly asking the retreatant to engage his imagination in prayer:

...when we contemplate Christ our Lord, the representation will consist in seeing with the vision of imagination
(*con la vista de la imaginacion*) the physical place (*el
lugar corpóreo*) where the matter we wish to contemplate
takes place. I said the physical place, for example, the temple, or the mountain where Jesus or his mother is...(47).

We notice how Ignatius focuses that imagination on the physical
(*corpóreo*) features of the event or person. In the final meditation on
hell, Ignatius asks the retreatant to exercise all the powers of his senses
upon that spiritual reality: "...to *see* in imagination the vast fires (66)
... to hear the wailing, the howling (67)...to smell the smoke, the sulfur
(68)...." (Again, the meditation closes with a dialogue with Jesus,
emphasizing gratitude for the retreatant's rescue.) This profoundly
physical "Application of the Senses" is suggested several times during
the *Exercises*. Let us then examine this most potent aspect of the
Exercises: the use of the imagination.

In *Christian Ethics and Imagination*, Philip Keane shows how
the imagination is a kind of faculty which unifies both sense and intellect in the individual. It relates universal and particular experiences. In
particular, he shows that "[i]magination also has a clear emotional element," and carries an inherent sense of appropriateness of passions
associated with particular symbols.[8] Keane's study allows us to see
more clearly why Ignatius wants the retreatant to engage her imagination in prayer. The central "symbol" in the *Exercises* is Jesus himself—the meeting place of human and divine passion, as Thomas
would say. Ignatius asks the retreatant to imagine Jesus and the con-
stellation of rich realities on his saving journey: Mary and Joseph, the
manger, the river Jordan, the mountain, Peter and John, Pilate and
Herod. Because the imagination has a "clear emotional element," the
retreatant's imagining of Jesus and his world engages her passions.
Because symbols carry an inherent sense of appropriateness of passions, the retreatant trains her passions by learning to feel with Jesus,
as Jesus feels. We find a profound sense of companionship and disci-
pleship here. We must be careful, then, when we call Jesus a "symbol"
in the *Exercises,* because we sometimes think of a symbol as different
from reality. Jesus is present to the retreatant, however, as a real person, with a real, even tangible presence more aptly described as the

"sacrament of the encounter with God."[9] The retreatant's sharing of passion with him is often imagistic, but not imaginary.

Ignatius has a purpose for placing the retreatant in such imaginative communion with Jesus. For Ignatius, the salvation accomplished by Jesus is not only a time-bound event, ending with the death and resurrection of Jesus some two thousand years ago. Ignatius sees Jesus' struggle for the reign of God as *still* occurring, and as occurring *now*, in the life and lifetime of the retreatant. When the retreatant imagines Jesus then, she is not only sharing in the first, paradigmatic struggle of Jesus. She is learning to re-envision her present world so she can imaginatively, creatively conform it to that paradigmatic mission of justice, liberation and love. By engaging her imagination, she is making herself available—in her senses, passions and intellect, as Keane tells us—to be moved by Jesus and to participate with him as he struggles now for her liberation, and for the liberation of all peoples in the reign of God on earth.[10]

The retreatant leaves the First Week then, with a profound sense of liberation, gratitude, and a growing desire to befriend this Jesus who has "set her free from the hands of all who persecute her" (Lk 1:71).

III. The Second Week: "Thy Kingdom Come. Thy Will Be Done on Earth...."

Ignatius centers the Second Week around two similar meditations which are the heart of the *Exercises*: "The Call of the King," and "The Two Standards."[11]

In the first part of "The Call of the King," the retreatant again engages his imagination, seeing the "synagogues, villages, and towns where Christ our Lord preached" (91). Then the retreatant is to reflect on the call of an "earthly king," chosen by God, who sincerely wants to right all the injustices in the world. Though the language may be foreign to the contemporary retreatant, the sense is not. We need only imagine how our hearts would rejoice to hear *any* political figure speak the truth about the poverty, homelessness and violence in our country. Suppose, then, that this same person had a realistic program (not false images and promises) that inspired us actually to *hope* for success. When I was in the Philippines, I listened over and over again to the pride and joy of the Filipinos who supported Corazon Aquino in the struggle against, and the eventual non-violent overthrow of, the Marcos regime. Ignatius has something like this experience in mind for the retreatant. Further, Ignatius' earthly king knows well the hardships that such a struggle for justice would entail, and he issues this invitation: "Whoever wishes to join with me in this enterprise must be content with the same food, drink, clothing, etc. as mine. So, too, he must work with me by day, and watch with me by night ..." (93, Puhl). Note again the powerful insistence on sharing, on interaction in that speech. The popular musical *Les Misérables* ends with the stirring invitation, "Will you join in our crusade? Who will be strong and stand with me? Somewhere beyond the barricades is there a world you long to see?" Ignatius would have loved it. He wants to stir the retreatant to share in the struggle for justice and peace, and in its glory.

Immediately after the call of the earthly ruler, the retreatant hears Jesus issue his own invitation to join with him—and is he not, Ignatius asks, more worthy of consideration? Again we see Ignatius redirecting our natural human passions (in this case, for justice) and lodging them in the passion for God. And again the human and divine passion meet in the person of Jesus. So Ignatius' chief purpose here is to establish an interactive relationship with Jesus by *sharing the good* of the reign of God: "...whoever wishes to join me in this enterprise must be willing to labor with me, that by following me in suffering, he may follow me in glory."[12] We recall from our study of Thomas that this sharing of goods is the central characteristic of friendship. Now, the shared good, the passion that unites both Jesus and the retreatant, will be the reign of God, where God "will pitch his tent among them, and they will be God's people.... God will wipe away every tear from their eyes, and there shall be no more death or mourning, crying out or pain" (Rev 21:3-4).

Placed together, the two parts of "The Call of the King" reinforce the deep insight that the reign of Jesus is very much a thing of *this world,* that his kingdom is to come *on earth* as it is in heaven. At the same depth, we see that Ignatius is "translating" passion and action. We know from our studies that the self is already in act by the very fact that it is in passion. Ignatius is saying here that the appropriate action in the passion for God is the struggle with Christ for the reign of God on earth. That action is appropriate, since it is the passion of

Christ to establish such a reign of justice and compassion, and the retreatant wants to feel with Christ.

This crucial meditation ends with Ignatius' suggested prayer for those who "wish to give greater proof of their love, and to distinguish themselves." Such persons will "not only offer themselves entirely for the work, but will act against their sensuality and carnal and worldly love, and make offerings of greater worth and more importance..." (97, Puhl). What does Ignatius intend by such a statement? We know by our study that he cannot mean the kind of Cartesian control that he himself has abandoned, nor the kind of body/spirit dichotomy that is no part of the *Exercises*. A story from Ignatius' *Autobiography* might illumine his meaning.

Long after he had committed himself entirely to God, Ignatius heard that a former companion of his (who had stolen his money) had fallen ill in Rouen, some eighty miles from Paris where Ignatius was staying. Ignatius "felt the desire to go to him and help him," and believed he could win him "entirely over to the service of God." Notice the astonishing range of passions as Ignatius describes his struggle to fulfill this desire:

> In order to obtain this [conversion] he felt the desire to walk the twenty-eight leagues from Paris to Rouen in his bare feet without eating or drinking. As he prayed for this he found that he was very much afraid.

Ignatius was afraid that he was putting God to the test by such extraordinary demands upon himself. But he prayed, and his fear of tempting God passed. He got up the next morning, though, and "As he began to dress, such a great fear came over him that he seemed almost unable to dress himself." He departed, but "still with that repugnance." The fear clutched at him as he journeyed, mile after mile, until Argenteuil, some nine miles from Paris. Then, Ignatius tells us,

> he passed the town with some spiritual travail, but as he climbed up a hill that fear began to go away. He felt great consolation and spiritual strength with such joy that he began to shout through the fields and to speak with God and so forth (*Auto*, 77).

For the record, Ignatius made it to Rouen in three days, barefoot and fasting the whole time, to comfort and aid his former companion. He then returned to Paris to face accusations from the Inquisition—but that is another story. Here, I would invite the reader to understand the *Spiritual Exercises,* and their training of the passions, in light of a person who could say that he woke in desolation—nearly paralyzed with fear. The same man can unabashedly describe how, later in the same day, he found himself in great consolation—*shouting* with joy, pursuing his goals with great energy, and speaking with God. Perhaps many of us can identify with Ignatius' pre-dawn feelings. But one of Ignatius' goals in the *Spiritual Exercises* is to teach us also how to speak with God, how to be empowered by our desires, and in the struggle to liberate God's people, how to shout with joy..."and so forth." Those, then, are the passions and actions of one who would "wish to distinguish himself" in the service of God.

We note again how Ignatius' lifelong struggle with his passions never led him to abandon them in exchange for a "cooler" or "more rational" state. Throughout his life, passions remain crucial to his spirituality. In this story, and in this meditation, however, Ignatius is giving the retreatant an insight which is often lacking in contemporary spirituality. We can find that insight clearly presented in Keane's book. Keane finds, for example, that many of his students view rape as a sexual problem and nothing more. However,

> such students cannot see that rape is profoundly connected
> to the way in which we organize society and to the many
> ways in which society systematically oppresses women.
> These students see rape only as the failure of certain isolat-
> ed individuals to control their sexual instincts (12).

Ignatius does see and experience that connection. Ignatius understands his struggles—and all such personal struggles—as the individual's partaking in the larger struggle *with Christ* to establish the reign of God. Ignatius sees that his efforts to help other people to the God of peace and justice will always be met with resistance, and that he will experience that resistance both exteriorly and interiorly. Ignatius sees himself as *struggling together with Christ* in these passions, for the establishment of the reign of God, against Christ's enemies. Overcoming the interior *and* exterior resistances toward the final goal (union of all creatures in God) would mean integration of the individual, *and* transformation of the network of *interactions* which form that individual. In this story, Ignatius sees that his personal triumph over depression inevitably means a step toward overcoming the *structural* oppression of sin; he sees the effort to overcome a structural oppression as necessarily involving a struggle for personal liberation. The meditations on the reign of God, then, are profoundly interactional in their understanding of the following of Jesus. They call for personal and structural struggles, in the friendship with Jesus whose shared gift is the reign of God.

The second great meditation of the Second Week of the *Exercises* reveals more of the shared passions and the shared mission of Jesus and the retreatant. It is the "Meditation on the Two Standards." Ignatius asks the participant to see the two cities, Jerusalem and Babylon, and to compare the "tactics" of the leaders of the two camps.

The retreatant first glances over the "field of battle," seeing Jesus as our "highest and true captain," and then Lucifer, "the robber-baron of all our enemies" (138). Each wants to win the world under his standard. The retreatant then imagines Lucifer, seated on a throne of fire and smoke, his appearance "horrible and terrifying" (140), sending out his demons to torment and chain up all those on earth. He tempts them to covet riches, then honor and recognition in the world, then to pride, and from those to "all the other vices" (142).

Then the retreatant turns her attention to Jesus who is in a "lowly place, His appearance beautiful and attractive." He chooses missionaries to send throughout the world, and then speaks to his servants and friends, "recommending to them that they desire to help all persons" (146) by attracting them to the way of God. There is an old revivalist hymn, called "Everybody Ought to Know." Its lyrics speak of Jesus: "He's the lily of the valley; He's the brightest morning star. He's the fairest of ten thousand. Everybody ought to know." Few of us, I believe, have paused to consider Jesus as physically attractive. Yet here, Ignatius is relying on the divine and human attractiveness of Jesus to capture all the retreatant's desires, and order them toward himself. The retreatant has Jesus as her *paradigmatic relationship*, not so much because as God he obliges her, but because he is so completely desirable, so utterly attractive that she is drawn toward him, moved by him. And by now she knows him—knows that he will not harm, knows that he liberates, blesses, heals—knows that "the bruised reed he will not break, the smoldering wick he will not quench, until he establishes justice on the earth.... And the distant islands await his law" (Is 42:2-3).

The retreatant also learns that the means have to be in keeping with the end, that the tactics of winning others to this lovely Lord have to be in keeping with his nature. So he hears his Lord speak to him about *attracting* others to the desire for poverty, reproaches, humility, and from there "encouraging them to all the other virtues" (146). Followers of Jesus are to be won not by force (for that is the tactic of Satan) but by love; not by the chains of compulsion, but by the beauty and attractiveness of Jesus, himself the way of God.

We cannot fail to notice the stark contrast, in both those meditations, between the kingdom of Christ and the kingdom of Satan. Why does Ignatius present us with such powerful disjunctive images? First, neither the gospels ("Whoever is not with me, is against me; whoever does not gather with me, scatters") nor Ignatius wishes to present the retreatant with any possibility of a lukewarm pledge, or middle ground that would weaken his commitment ("You are the salt of the earth...but if the salt loses its savor..."). Further, the clarity of these two meditations provides a welcome antidote to the paralyzing "confusion" which is characteristic of hell, as we saw in the First Week. The confusion of that hell is nowhere more apparent than in the mentally ill, who have, according to Lynch, lost the "*taste* of themselves,"[13] and so have become hopelessly trapped and confused, unable to *act* because of constant internal and external contradictions which "stalemate" them.[14] Ignatius, no stranger himself to the passions characteristic of depression, writes about the evil spirit:

> It is characteristic of the evil one to fight against such happiness and consolation by proposing fallacious reasonings, subtleties, and continual deception...thus he seeks to prevent the soul from advancing.[15]

Finally, Ignatius submits that the passions which are engaged in these exercises in imagining, or which are engaged in the struggle for the reign of God, can come from relationship with forces from outside: with evil spirits, or with good spirits. And the *incipient purposive actions* which are passions must be *discerned* so that the retreatant can tell which relationship is prompting those actions. We have referred earlier to the *consolations* and *desolations* of the *Exercises*. Put simply, consolations are passions which are in harmony with the paradigmatic relationship with Jesus, and desolations are passions in disharmony with it.[16] Thus, in those two meditations, Ignatius is leading the retreatant to direct spiritual experience of the principles of discernment. Ignatius expects that the retreatant will always be moved throughout his life in passion. The retreatant can test all those passions, then, for their *resonance* with the experience of union and mission with Jesus.

IV. An Important Aside: The Body in *The Spiritual Exercises*

Ignatius' "Application of the Senses" in the meditation on hell, the Christmas story, and throughout the *Exercises*, should draw our attention to his extraordinary emphasis on the body. In the opening Annotation, Ignatius draws the parallel between physical and spiritual exercises (*SE*, 1). Ignatius also sets great value on the consolation of tears in prayer, since the evidence of the body being moved was for him evidence that the spirit was being moved.[17] We can also see that in the consolation of tears, the body is acting "in sympathetic vibration" with the spirit. And if the spirit is engaged in contemplation of the things of God, then, as Thomas would say, "the body, too, shares in spiritual things" when we weep. With such tears then, the body itself is being purified and sanctified: "My heart *and my flesh* rejoice in the living God" (Ps 83).

Both Thomas and Ignatius share, then, a concern for the body in passion, and particularly in the passion for God. For Ignatius, that concern is first and primarily because he wants to have the retreatant relate to Jesus *incarnate* through the power of the Holy Spirit, and the only appropriate human engagement with that Lord in the Holy Spirit is as embodied.[18]

Ignatius, however, has a more modern understanding of the body as a source of each person's *individual identity,* and he wants to use that understanding to encourage each retreatant to have her own unique way of relating with the Lord in the passion of prayer.[19] So for example, later in the *Exercises* he writes that diet, sleep and penances are to be altered until the retreatant finds what he desires from God, "for since God our Lord knows our nature infinitely well, he frequently grants appropriate graces so that each one (*cado uno*) can sense (*sentir*) what is fitting (*conviene*) for him" (89).[20]

That observation brings us to another insight. We recall Thomas' fondness for the line from Psalm 83, "My heart and my flesh rejoice in the living God." Ignatius also knows this passion. It is the sense that the self is attuned, soul and body, to God, who is our deepest joy. Ignatius' word for this integrated (spirit and body), interrelational, and distinctively personal passion is *sentir*. We know from studies discussed in this book that we are always being affected by others. But notice how that reality becomes most useful in our relationships with those most important to us. It explains why, without words, spouses— and even some college roommates who are close—can "just know" when the other is in joy or in sorrow. This same "sense" (*sentir*) of being moved in "sympathetic vibration" *with Christ* is, it seems to me, the central goal and passion of the *Exercises*, akin to the *joy* that Thomas describes as the highest passion in the moral life. Thus after describing "consolation" in different ways, Ignatius concludes that consolation is "every interior joy which calls and draws a person toward heavenly things and toward her personal salvation (*la propria salud*), giving her *quies* and rest (*quietandola y pacificandola*) in her Creator and Lord."[21] Thomas had indicated in the *Treatise on the Passions* that such communion was possible. Here, with his attention to the unique passions and bodily needs of the retreatant, Ignatius enables the retreatant to realize Thomas' insight: to enjoy in his own flesh an interpersonal relationship with the God who can become his closest companion, his friend in the incarnate Christ.

An interesting thing happens to the meaning of the body from the beginning to the end of the journey of the *Exercises*. In the First Week meditations on sin and hell, Ignatius asks the retreatant to "consider my soul to be incarcerated in this corruptible body" (47). Ignatius tells him this precisely because he understands such a condition to be characteristic of *sin;* it is a deformity of the human condition to have the spirit at war with the body. But in the culminating contemplation of the

Exercises, the "Contemplation to Embrace Love," we find Ignatius encouraging the retreatant to consider how God dwells in creatures, giving existence to all, vegetation to plants, sense perception to animals—"And how He dwells in me as well, giving me existence, movement, sense perception, and empowering me to understand, thus making a temple of me, who am created in the likeness and image of the Divine Majesty" (235). There we note the complete reversal of sin and its disintegrative effects, so much so that sense perception itself is seen as a result of God's presence to the retreatant. The entire person is compared to a temple of God, and the lost sense of being in the "image and likeness" of God is restored. Thus, as Brun tells us, "The body... is integrated into the life of prayer, into the life of faith, to decisions and choice. Meditated upon, contemplated on, the word of God gradually transforms the being of flesh that is who we are."[22]

And we see in that same "Contemplation to Embrace Love" that Ignatius wants the retreatant to understand his particular humanity in the world in the way Thomas has suggested: as mediator between the world of the spirit and the corporeal world. The wording of the prayer establishes a connection between the retreatant and all creation. The personal experience of the redemption of his own embodied reality through the love of Christ, extends, through that very same embodiment, to the embodied world which her Redeemer has created and redeemed.[23] Ignatius himself experienced this interrelatedness between himself and all creation. In describing a day of prayer in his *Journal,* he first finds a deep "loving humility" for the Creator, and then, later in the day, "I had much joy in remembering this, and I thought that I should not stop there, but the same would be true later of creatures, that is, loving humility..." (243).

The body, then, as a principle of individuality, was in danger of becoming a "wall," dichotomized from the soul, and excluding the other. But by the end of the *Exercises,* the meaning of the body has been transformed. By the end of the journey with Jesus, the body is seen as the integrated source of personal identity, and as the way of being interrelated with all others, because the embodied person partakes of the passions that all creatures share for their "Creator and Lord."[24]

Ignatius wants the retreatant to experience still another meaning

of the body in passion, and we will see that more clearly when we turn
to the meditations of the Third Week.

V. The Third Week: "Were You There When They Crucified My Lord?"

Our discussion of the body in passion with Jesus brings us naturally to the discussion of the Third Week of the *Exercises*. All this
week, the retreatant meditates on the suffering and death of Jesus—
archetypically called "the passion" of Christ. More profoundly than
any other time, Ignatius wants the retreatant to immerse himself in this
passion, "For in the Passion all His virtues shine out far more conspic-
uously and gloriously, and more powerfully invite us to imitate Him"
(*Dir.*, Ch. XXV, 1).

After again asking the retreatant to recall the history, and to
imagine the physical place,[25] Ignatius tells the retreatant to ask for the
passions of "sorrow, compassion and shame because the Lord is going
to His suffering for my sins" (*SE* 193, Puhl). Upon hearing of Jesus'
betrayal and suffering at the last supper, "I should begin to struggle
with great effort to strive to grieve, be sad and to weep" (195). And
later, in the contemplation on the agony in the garden, the retreatant
should "ask for sorrow with Christ in sorrow, anguish with Christ in
anguish, tears and deep grief..." (203). Once again we hear Ignatius'
emphasis that we must be moved as Jesus is moved, and again we hear
echoes of Thomas, who tells us that it is morally good to be sad about
evil things.

Viard is most helpful to us in understanding the appropriate passions that Ignatius seeks in the Third Week. He writes that, like the
apostles, we are reluctant to join in the passion of our Lord, and so
must strive to "reduce the distance which separates us from the suffering Christ" and so "search out and find compassion for Him."[26] Viard's
first idea is quite instructive since Ignatius often suggests that, when
we find reluctance to the "right" passions, we *act against that reluctance.*

Here is a crucial feature of the morality of the passions to which
we have only been alluding thus far. We want to feel "in the right way,
at the right time, to the right extent." But what if we don't? What is the

best way to *change* our passions so that we *do* feel "the right way"? Ignatius has told us that to feel the right way is to feel with Jesus. Throughout the *Exercises*, and here specifically, he gives us the means to change our passions. We can change our passions not by exercising the mind's control over the body or the passions, but by *earnestly asking Jesus* to grant the desires and passions we want.[27] Passions, which are constitutively interactive, cannot be changed by the self alone. They must be changed interactively. I know from my own experience that when I feel jealous of a friend's success, my passion changes when I go to my friend and confess that I am feeling jealous, and can he help and pray with me? Ignatius tells us that when we are feeling the wrong way, we should go to Jesus our best friend, and earnestly ask that, from within that paradigmatic relationship, he change our passions by drawing them more toward himself. Paul writes, "But if *by the Spirit* you put to death the works of the flesh, you will live" (Rom 8:13). Of course this will require time, as we have seen in our study. But our passions become neither moral nor holy by some kind of suppression or Cartesian control. They become holy through our habitual communion with Jesus, through our passion for God.

Viard's second point is also suggestive. If, as we have been implying in our study, the interrelationship *with Christ* is *mutual*, then there must be some time during the journey of the *Spiritual Exercises* when Christ's *need for the retreatant* becomes apparent. And that does occur, in the Third Week, during the passion. In the same way as Jesus called for support from the apostles ("My soul is sorrowful, even to death; remain here and watch with me" [Mt 26:38]), now I see that Jesus needs *my com-passion*, for he is to suffer, and for *my* sins.[28]

Schellenberger is particularly sensitive to that call for compassion and the mutuality and union it entails. He writes:

> The compassion described is not a standing apart, but an experience of becoming one flesh, one organic unity, profoundly and fundamentally bound together. The bond is physical: one's own "gut-feeling" and "gut-knowledge" arouses a presence for, and defense of, the other, since what happens to the other is felt in my own flesh and blood.[29]

Now, too, the mission of the reign of God is made more clear, more personal, and more interactive with Jesus, for Jesus tells us in Matthew 25, "*I* was hungry and you gave me food; *I* was thirsty and you gave me drink...." The physical reality and bonding between Jesus and the retreatant now extends to all, and especially to the oppressed.

Finally, this changing of the meaning of suffering changes the meaning of the body for the retreatant. The retreatant is more and more being transformed by her love of *Christ crucified*, and this is becoming the central symbol in her life, as suggested in the epigraph to this chapter. When we look for an illustration of that transformation, we find that Ignatius himself presents us with what might otherwise be a puzzling story in the *Autobiography*. Spanish soldiers have taken Ignatius as a spy while he was on one of his pilgrimages. They strip-search him, looking through "all the parts of his body" for the "message" he must be carrying. Then,

> unable to learn anything by any means, they bound him to take him to the captain, who would make him talk.... On the way the pilgrim saw a kind of *representation* of Christ being led away, but this was *not a vision like the others*. He was taken through three main streets, and he went without any sadness, but rather with joy and contentment (*Auto.* 55).

What was that *representation* which was "not a vision like the others"? Throughout the *Autobiography*, Ignatius had already given several examples of what a vision of Jesus was like.[30] This experience, however, was different. Here, he sees his suffering in *his* arrest as *representing* the suffering of Christ in *his* arrest. That "imaging" in his own self the "image of the unseen God," that incarnating in *his* body what Jesus incarnated, that "profound and fundamental bond" by which he sensed himself "following and imitating" (*sequendo y imitando*) Christ, or, more simply, that warm companionship of these two friends in "poverty, insult and humility" (*pobreza, vituperación y humildad*) gave Ignatius "not sorrow, but rather joy and contentment." And it is that meaning of the body, its passions and its sufferings, that Ignatius most wants to share in this Third Week: that we are the body of Christ. The retreatant will need this insight, not only because he wants to bond more closely with Jesus, but also because the struggle to establish the reign of justice and compassion—the struggle to feed Christ hungry and to give drink to Christ thirsty—will require him also to suffer, even to die. In this Week, however, the retreatant feels the liberating and healing power of his own suffering as he struggles and suffers with Jesus.[31] Such shared passion for the reign of God will bring him "not sorrow, but rather joy and contentment."

VI. The Fourth Week: The "Ode to Joy"

Joy was, for Thomas, the consummate rational passion. In the Fourth Week meditations on the Easter experiences, the retreatant is to "ask for the grace that I might celebrate and rejoice intensely at such glory and joy of Christ our Lord" (221). He begins with "remembering" the resurrection and imagining the concrete place of the appearances (228-29). When he awakes, he turns his mind to the contemplation at hand, and "seeks to have himself affected and rejoicing" at such great joy and happiness of Christ our Lord. The retreatant must not think of sad things; he must use light and seasons to help him in his rejoicing.

There is a new quality of friendship in the Fourth Week, of shared joy in the good of the risen Jesus, and we can see it most clearly by focusing the culminating prayer of the *Exercises,* the *Contemplation for Attaining Love.* There the themes of mutuality, particularity, embodiment, and transformation are all unified.

The Prelude to the Contemplation states that love "ought to present itself more in works than in words," reminding us of the importance of the body, and of its action. Ignatius next states, "Love consists in a communication between two parts...the one who loves communicates to the beloved whatever he or she can and the beloved in return to the lover" (232).

There, Ignatius gives us his strongest presentation of the mutuality of love which he wishes for the Lord and the retreatant. He is first of all intentionally unclear about the *referents* of "the lover" and "the beloved." Is the retreatant reaching out to God's love, or is God reaching out to the retreatant's love? Both.[32] Then Ignatius tells us that, after pondering "with much affection"[33] the many gifts which God our Lord has given to me, I should know that "the same Lord desires to give Himself to me as much as He can, according to divine ordering."[34]

Always, Ignatius has asked the retreatant to "ask for what she desires" in the *Exercises*. Now we finally see clearly what *God* desires: not just to give gifts, but to give God's own very Self to me. Again we discover a mutuality between God and the retreatant. Ignatius has first shown us that our affections and desires[35] must be ordered by lodging them entirely in the relationship with God in Jesus. Now we find that God's desires to "give God's own very Self to me" are divinely ordered by emptying the fullness of God's own self into the person of Jesus, the meeting place of divine and human passion.

We already expect what Ignatius will ask the retreatant next: that the retreatant should consider how he should offer back to God "everything I have, and myself together with them,"[36] sharing goods as friends do, fulfilling the mutual bond of friendship with God in Christ. Here the retreatant most completely accepts Jesus and his struggle for the reign of justice and compassion.

Ignatius also has the retreatant consider how God dwells in creatures, giving them existence, vegetation, sense and intellect, as we have seen in Thomas. He asks the retreatant to

> consider how God works and labors for me in all created things on the face of the earth, that is, God acts in the manner of one who is laboring. For example, God is working in the heavens, elements, plants, fruits, cattle...(236).

That is an echo of the phrasing of the First Week, except that now the retreatant sees that, in all creation, "My Father works, and I am working still"—and that is another way the retreatant can find joy in the presence of the risen Jesus. Like my friend delighting and then rejoicing in that ripe tomato, we see that God works "by granting being, by preserving them, concurring with their vegetative and sensate activities, and so forth...." This is not a love of mere gazing upon. If the retreatant wants to *labor with Christ*, she must labor as Christ labors. That cannot be done by violative force, but by working creatively from within, toward the creature's own end, as the Creating Word works.[37]

Among Ignatius' followers, the phrase which refers to that insight of God working through his creatures is "finding God in all things," and of our sharing in the joyful mission of the risen Christ, being "a contemplative in action." Put another way, "God is discovered as interior to the soul just as God is interior to things." In that mission, the retreatant is to consider that all gifts descend from above, even "my own limited powers." That is another way that Jesus shares the dance of the resurrection with the retreatant: the retreatant begins to see that not only her consolation, but all her gifts, "justice, goodness, piety, compassion," come from the paradigmatic passion for God in Christ. In that way, though she does not yet have the fullness of the resurrection, the retreatant nevertheless "walks in the newness of life," finding her joy in God within, and in all things.

With this, the culminating meditation of the Fourth Week—and of the whole *Spiritual Exercises*—the retreatant is sent rejoicing into the world, a world which is "charged with the grandeur of God," to labor in love with Jesus for the coming of the reign of God. Jesuits sometimes call that labor the "Fifth Week" of the *Exercises*. Let us then turn to our final chapter and see how a passion for God might work itself out as a passion for justice.

6.

A PASSION FOR JUSTICE

If you don't think about it, you won't be sad.

—Anonymous

If the one giving the Exercises notices that the person making them...is not being moved one way or another by different spirits, the director should question the retreatant much about the Exercises....   —Ignatius

In keeping with the themes of this book, I want to focus our discussion of justice in a particular way. I want to focus on the body—on the sacredness of the body, and the concomitant right to live without violation of one's body, or the fear of that violation. More specifically, I want to concentrate on the kind of physical violence that arises when a self is trying to assert dominance over an other. Such a discussion will reveal the passions that can be formed into the virtue of non-violence. Finally, as an image of the just community, I find no better portrait than that of Rosemary Radford Ruether. "In God's Kingdom the corrupting principles of domination and subjugation will be overcome. People...will discover a new kind of power, a power exercised through service, which empowers the disinherited and brings all to a new relationship of mutual enhancement."[1]

I. The Temptation Not To Be Moved

We began this book with the story of Fabian, moved by the plight of his "little brother," who had been a victim of abuse. I would like to begin our final discussion by setting Fabian's story off against a few other stories, to observe the effect of *not* being moved.

In one segment of his PBS special, war historian Gwynne Dyer interviews two young men who have just executed a training drill. They have gone through the firing sequence that would launch a nuclear-armed ballistic missile from its silo to its target. As they turn the keys, Dyer intones, "This is the way the world will end." Later, he asks them, "Is it automatic now?" One of the crew, a young blond with horn-rimmed glasses, responds, "At this point, we're hoping for a 'yes' vote from another two man crew to launch the missile.... After that it's automatic." Dyer asks, "How would you feel if you ever had to do it for real?" The young man responds that they are so highly trained in simulators like this every month that their response is pretty much automatic. Dyer offers, "You wouldn't be thinking about it at the time," and the young man continues respectfully, "There wouldn't be time for any reflection until after we turned the keys and waited for the indications [that the missiles were launched]." Dyer persists, "Would there be reflection then, do you think?" The young man presents the camera with the most beatific smile: "I should think so," he acknowledges, nodding, "Yes."

As I have reflected on the passions through the years, I have also come to see how we fall victim to the temptation *not* to be moved in our culture. In fact, this lack of passion is often cultivated, with incalculably destructive results. In our recounting of the TV interview above, we see that the young soldiers are "highly trained" not to feel, not to be moved by the hundreds of thousands of deaths they would be causing. Perhaps we might excuse them, thinking that the mind and heart become numb at the prospect of uncountable dead. But the problem seems more pervasive in our culture than that.

At one time or another, the reader has probably heard someone say the quote which begins this chapter. I found it in another story, this time about the killing of a single person, a seven year old girl. A group of young children had been playing a Nintendo game. One of the young girls bragged to her nine year old playmate that she could beat him at this particular game, now that her parents had purchased it for her, and she could practice at home. A few moments later, the father told all the children that they had to go outside to play. The little girls went outside to play on the snowmobile, while the nine year old boy returned to his parents' house next door. There, "according to testimony, he went to his parents' second-floor bedroom and reached inside the base of a lamp to get the key to his father's gun cabinet." He then

> unlocked the cabinet and from the 10 rifles there picked
> out a 35-caliber Marlin with a sling and scope.... The
> police say that [he] then unlocked an ammunition drawer,
> found the right bullets, loaded the rifle, climbed on the bed,
> opened the window and removed the screen.

He shot his seven year old playmate with the Marlin, then replaced the rifle, hid the spent bullet in the case of unused bullets and returned downstairs.

At that point, the father of the young girl who had been shot telephoned and told the young boy to return to the house, since there appeared to be a sniper on the loose. According to several people, the young boy returned and "walked past the living room where [the young girl] lay dying and turned the video game back on, telling the other children, 'If you don't think about it, you won't be sad.'"[2]

As painful as such stories are, they seem to confirm the interactive model that we have been developing in this book. The young boy (and all who have undertaken the same strategy) seemed to sense the integrated relationship between thinking and feeling: he knew that if he did not think, he would not feel. We might also get a glimpse of the nature of his passions when we observe the others with whom he has been relating. His father, a laborer, had ten rifles. If we can assume that it was the father who taught the son how to load and shoot, then the rifles would have acquired a special *meaning* for the boy. They would have been an important way of interacting with his father. They would have been one of those "goods exchanged" through which Thomas would say a "love-of-friendship" was established. Thomas would further point out that the quality of the relationship, and the quality of the persons *in* the relationship, would be determined by the nature of the goods exchanged.

If we look again at the young boy's interactions, we discover that the nature of the video game he was playing requires the player to kill spies in order to score points. The more killing, the more points. Constant interaction with such a game *trains* one in certain ways. It seems we are often blind to the effect of such training. The article notes that the young boy celebrated his tenth birthday while awaiting trial for murder. It closes by telling us that, as a birthday present, "His parents gave him a Nintendo game."

I am not saying that we have discovered all the causes of the young boy's behavior. I am using this difficult example to highlight the danger of not feeling, of not being moved. I want also to point out that such passion-less behavior—especially with regard to violence—is an unfortunate characteristic of our modern culture. Examples could be multiplied. During the Gulf War, Philip Shenon interviewed Captain Mike Sanders of the Army's Second Armored Division. Sanders explained, "Our mission is a destruction mission. We are to expend the ammunition and time it takes to destroy the enemy forces." After noting that "the killing will be extensive," Sanders added that, "after the war is over, maybe I can philosophize on whether that was right."[3] Terry Leonard recently interviewed a sniper in the war in Bosnia. "I try not to think about it," the twenty year old told him. "I try to cut myself off from my feelings." Though later she noted, "When I shoot, I see what I did. It is very personal. I don't know how this will affect me later." Her commander agreed. "We all try to cut off our emotions. We are afraid we will end up in some kind of hospital or mental ward when the war ends."[4]

That inability to be moved is the ultimate danger of the prevailing model of the morality of affectivity: to "be strong" and unaffected. We see that there has occurred what Robert Jay Lifton has called "doubling," defined as "the division of the self into two functioning wholes, so that a part-self acts as an entire self." And there we hear the echo of the Cartesian-based philosophers of Chapter 2. Reflecting on the activities of the Nazi doctors, Lifton says that they entered into a "Faustian bargain with the diabolical environment" in exchange for "various psychological and material benefits."[5] Part of the dynamic of doubling Lifton calls "psychic numbing"—or the inability to feel. Even in such a place as professional football, we hear about the essential dynamic of psychic numbing in response to violence. In an interview, John Frank, who finally quit professional football to pursue a career as a doctor, said, "For many years I desensitized myself. I kept pushing my feelings back and back, repressing any sort of human emotion, especially when I saw an injury....A lot of players have these feelings, but they never speak about them."[6]

In an interview, Peter Hagelstein tells of his leaving weapons work at the Livermore Laboratory. The laboratory promised him that he could have a laboratory X-ray laser for medical work, in exchange for guidance on the X-ray laser weapon. Interestingly, Hagelstein uses the same language as Lifton: "It was a hard, personal compromise I made: A Faustian bargain. And it wasn't worth it—not even close."[7] And yet such violations of the essentially relational nature of the self, and of its concomitant movement toward integration, can never be complete. In the interview, Hagelstein speaks constantly of his nightmares. Then, in a particularly revealing passage, he tells us,

> So you close your eyes and mind and don't worry about weapons work. You go on—more sleepless nights. There was a time when two nights out of the week I couldn't fall asleep at all. You lose your health; you develop high blood pressure, heart problems. You collapse at the pool, get hauled into the Livermore medical center, and asked if you work for the feudal lords of the laser program who regularly send their people in on stretchers.[8]

In all this, we see evidence of the numbness of violent behavior; in the last instance, we see negative evidence of the mind-body integration and the disintegrative cost of denying passions. As we said in Chapter 2, the self and the other can be destroyed, but are not infinitely malleable in interaction. If it is the nature of the self to be moral, then we see that the self violates itself in preparing weapons that violate another. And though such evidence is anecdotal, there is no end to the hard evidence of the pervasiveness of violence especially in North American culture. Prothrow-Stith begins her book, *Deadly Consequences*, with a series of alarming statistics.

> The overall homicide rate of 21.9 per 100,000 for young males in the United States was between 4 and 73 times higher than the homicide rate for young males in any other industrialized nation. In Austria, for example, the homicide rate for young males was .3. In Japan the figure was .5. In

Germany, Denmark and Portugal the figure was 1.0—less than one-twentieth of the American figure.[9]

The reasons for this violence are many. For this chapter, I would like to adopt and focus on the feminist critique of *power*. Most feminists critique the patriarchal view of power as hierarchical, competitive and exclusivistic, and they have assembled a convincing body of evidence to support their claims. In her illuminating study, *In Memory of Her* for example, Schüssler Fiorenza displays the roots of this thinking in western thought. It is particularly painful to reread such classic texts as Aristotle's *Politics* through the eyes of a sister theologian. Schüssler Fiorenza quotes Aristotle at length as he argues that "the male is by nature better fitted to command than the female" (*Politics* I.1259b), and shows the parallel between that position and his understanding that slavery is ordained by nature.[10] Her work shows how Judaic and Hellenistic views of patriarchy and power encroached upon, then gradually overcame the egalitarianism characteristic of the early Christian church. When Radford Ruether seeks to recover the scriptural prophetic spirit for the feminist project, she rightly sees that spirit as "destabilizing toward the existing social order and its hierarchies of power—religious, social, and economic."[11]

The chief purpose of these and other feminist studies is to claim, or reclaim, the rightful place of women in our world. In this chapter, I am using their analysis of power in a slightly different, though I am sure, relevant, way. I see the understanding of power as hierarchical, competitive and exclusivistic to be the theoretical undergirding for the injustice of violence which so plagues our world. Such an understanding of power prevents passion as we have been presenting it in this book, precisely because it precludes mutuality. "For within living structures defined by profit, by linear power, by institutional dehumanization, our feelings were not meant to survive."[12] Such an understanding of the power of the self looks upon the other as an intrusion into the sphere of the self, especially if the other is claiming any kind of equality with the self—and so reacts with repudiation.[13] And whether we agree or not that violence is gender-specific, we cannot argue with the conclusion of Prothrow-Stith, "While much about human aggression is not known, one fact is indisputable: Among all races, all classes, and in every corner of the globe men are more violent than women"

(9). I am particularly concerned, in the context of this study, to discover in this chapter what might be the central passion for males, such that men give up their false understanding of power, and the violence toward the other required to enforce that understanding. What would move us, then, and move us toward non-violence?

II. The Redemption from Violence: The Capacity To Be Moved

Melissa Everett's *Breaking Ranks* is a compilation of stories of men who have left their jobs in the military or intelligence communities to work for peace. As we hear her interviewees describe the process of their emerging from this numbing, we also find movements similar to those we have been observing in this book. Jerry Genesio lost a brother in Vietnam. His journey toward peace began when he realized that much of the blood imported to the U.S. came from the Nicaraguan poor, where it was bought for about a dollar, and sold for about thirty in the U.S. It was nearly complete when he went to Nicaragua years later in the Witness for Peace program. In front of a crowd of Nicaraguans and visiting North Americans, Genesio began to "tell the story of his brother's death, and his own years of reconciliation." He says, "I remember telling that story and crying, having a hard time getting it all out. For the first time in fifteen years, I felt whole."[14]

We notice the importance of weeping in Genesio's account and the resultant sensation of being whole, as opposed to the numbing and doubling spoken of by Lifton and others. We might also claim, in keeping with the themes of this book, that Genesio's grief at the loss of his brother was *in his body*, and that he could never be whole until he acknowledged that grief in a physical way. We recall the emphasis on the spiritually transformative power of weeping in the spirituality of Ignatius. We see the same emphasis on the ability to "be moved" in story after story. Ralph McGehee was working for the CIA in Vietnam and became more and more convinced that "the U.S. was kidding itself and his intelligence work was helping it do so" until finally "[i]n the silence punctuated occasionally by the bombing outside, the former Notre Dame football hero sat and sobbed.... And from that evening of despair, a resolve crystallized in his mind: to stay alive to do something, somehow, to compensate for the damage he had contributed to…(56). David MacMichael quit his job working for the CIA. During his time of transition, a staff member at the Nuevo Instituto de Centro America, Joanne Sunshower, noticed: "He seemed to be paying a lot of attention to the quality of his personal relationships…. He was allowing himself to be moved" (77). John Graham was a CIA officer who worked in Libya and Vietnam. In the course of his conversion, he was telling war stories to

> a group of thirty men in a workshop which addressed the Jungian concept of "masculine" and "feminine" in the human personality. Abruptly, the group leader said, "Okay, I want you all to pick out the man in this room who you think is the most feminine." Thirty men pointed to Graham, who ran out of the room as if he had been given a death sentence.

Soon, though, Graham understood: "There was a side of him that was spiritual, intuitive, capable of being deeply moved. It occurred to him that his attraction to violence was somehow connected to his suppression of that part of himself" (95).

We can see from the above examples that a primary feature for those moving away from violence and militarism is some experience of being moved. But this is not yet the full account, since we must be moved in the right way, at the right time, etc. Let us continue our study then of this right experience of being moved toward justice, and, in particular, the right passion for the virtue of non-violence.

III. A Passion for Non-Violence

Recently, I was in Israel-Palestine with some two hundred people from twenty countries on a "Walk for a Peaceful Future in the Middle East." We had come from all over the world to support those peace groups who were working in accordance with UN resolutions for a two-state solution to the Israeli-Palestinian problem. We were also calling for both communities to forswear violence, and for an end to the Israeli occupation of the Palestinian people, which the Israelis must

enforce with human rights violations, and with torture. We all had
pledged ourselves to non-violence in deed, word and thought.

At a particular point in the walk, we arrived at the so-called
"Green Line"—an invisible division between Israel and its occupied
territories. We were intending to walk to support peace groups which
had invited us to join them in the occupied territories. The Israeli government took exception to that, and forbade us to cross the Green Line.
They lined up scores of border police, with jeeps and vans and buses to
carry us away if we approached the Line. They all had automatic
weapons. Then they brought out four horses and lined them up opposite us, their riders armed with pistols and protected with bulletproof
vests. We were given five minutes to clear the field and withdraw, or
they would "evacuate" us.

Most of us decided to continue the walk, and were quietly
preparing for our encounter with the massed military. Significantly,
this was to be a physical encounter. This group had decided to go
beyond writing letters, or even demonstrating in front of the UN. We
had decided on a physical presence to the Israeli and Palestinian peace
groups, and a physical engagement with the military. As I moved
through the walkers, I became attuned to two passions. First, we were
characterized by a certain serenity and then, from within that serenity,
moved by a kind of *eagerness* toward our engaging with the military.
There was a freshness about this eagerness which transcended the fact
that we were tired and dirty from being on the road for days. The
eagerness was not the impatience of wanting to get it over with, and
still less the lust of trying to dominate someone. It seemed more like
the eagerness of lovers.

It seems to me that this eagerness, this willingness to encounter
and undergo physical suffering, is the primary passion for the virtue of
non-violence. Like all passions, this passion must be trained—and this
passion especially, lest it become a wrong passion, a passion for self-
destruction. But before we speak of its training, let us search for this
passion for suffering especially among those committed to non-violence. We do not need to read very far in Gandhi's work to see the
value he places on "self-suffering." He says, for example, that
"Suffering in one's own person is...the essence of nonviolence and is
the chosen substitute for violence to others."[15] As another example, we
recall that on January 30, 1956, the house of Martin and Coretta King

was bombed, and Coretta, Yolanda, and Mrs. Denise Roscoe, wife of a church member, narrowly escaped injury. When an angry crowd gathered around the King house, armed and calling for vengeance, King sent them home in peace. According to Andrew Young, King's refusal to accept retaliatory violence at that time definitively stamped the character of non-violence on the civil rights movement.[16]

More pointedly, this passion to accept suffering into the self is characteristic of Jesus who was crucified. Luke's gospel highlights this when Jesus says, "I have come to bring fire to the earth, and how I wish it were blazing already! There is a baptism I must still receive, and how I wish it were already completed!" (12:49-50). The letter to the Hebrews tells us that Jesus "endured the cross, despising the shame" (12:2). And Christians are commanded to take up the cross as Jesus did and to suffer as he suffered. If I am right in this understanding, Christians are therefore invited to join Jesus in his non-violent passion for justice. Since "the one who is in us is more powerful than the one who is in the world," Christians can rely on this inner power to absorb, as it were, and overcome the lesser power of violence and domination. That is why we do not "fight directly against evil, but overcome evil with good."

There has been much discussion about the possibility of distinctively Christian passions. In the *Spiritual Exercises*, Ignatius in the meditation on the Two Standards encourages the retreatant to passions which, apart from interaction with Jesus, would surely seem outlandish.

> Consider the address which Christ our Lord makes to all his servants and friends whom he is sending on this mission. He recommends that they endeavor to aid all persons, by attracting them, first to the highest degree of spiritual poverty and also, if his Divine Majesty would be served and pleased to choose them for it, to no less a degree of actual poverty; second, by attracting them to a *desire of reproaches and contempt,* since from these results humility (146, emphasis added).

Ignatius himself never completed the journey to the virtue of non-violence. Here, however, he has revealed distinctively Christian

(and attractive!) passions which are essential in the mission for peace
and justice. And they are distinctively Christian because they are
shared *with Christ,* as Ignatius indicates earlier in the *Exercises*:

> My will is to conquer the whole world and all my enemies,
> and thus to enter into the glory of my Father. Therefore,
> whoever wishes to come *with me* must labor *with me* so
> that through *following me* in the pain he or she may *follow
> me* also in the glory (95, emphasis added).

Here, by using "with me" twice, and "follow me" twice, Ignatius
preserves the mystery of Jesus. Jesus shares with us the passion for
suffering. He suffered in his own body, and continues to suffer in his
body, the church. Through him, our passion for suffering—our passion
for justice—is caught up in our passion for God. That is why Ignatius
told the story of his re-presenting Jesus' suffering in himself, and then
told us that such suffering brought him "not sorrow, but joy and contentment." It is that same distinctively Christian passion which the
apostles experienced after they had been flogged, "And so they
left...*glad* to have had the honor of suffering humiliation for the sake
of the name" (Acts 5:41).

In the sermon on the mount in Matthew, Jesus tells the crowd
that they should rejoice when people abuse them and persecute them
(5:11-12). He also says, "Blessed are those who suffer persecution for
the sake of justice, theirs is the reign of heaven" (5:10). The Vulgate
there is "Beati qui persecutionem patiuntur propter iustitiam...." I
think of Gandhi, of Ignatius, and of my friends from all over the world
gathered at the Green Line. And I wonder what the effect would be on
our understanding of justice and non-violence if we were to translate
that beatitude as, "Blessed are those who have a passion for persecution for the sake of justice...."

IV. A Passion for Justice

In our discussion of non-violence, we need to make a careful
observation, again to protect the self from disintegration or erasure. We
can make that observation concretely at first by telling what non-vio-

lence is not. A child being beaten by her caretaker(s) is not non-violent. A spouse acceding to physical abuse is not non-violent.[17] A people accepting domination by another people or government is not non-violent. Even more, a person standing by while others are victimized by oppression is not non-violent. What is characteristically non-violent about non-violence is precisely that it refuses to accept violence as a feature of interrelationships. For that reason, non-violence must be seen as bound up with a passion for justice in order to be authentic. Let us discuss the interplay of the passion for non-violence, and the passion for justice.

For Thomas, the passion most immediately associated with justice was *anger*.[18] J. Giles Milhaven has studied this passion for justice. He rightly points out that: "That violent impulse, this foggy urge to hit back, is...a lunge of the person, *both mind and body*, for justice."[19] However, his victim-centered approach to "good anger" does not quite address the violence we are considering here, and his failure to consider the dehumanizing effects of violence causes him too many difficulties.[20] Here we are considering the violence inherent in the patriarchal view of power, and from the perspective of those who are by their violence exercising domination over an other. That is by far the most common form of the all too common phenomenon of violence. And we have said that what seems most characteristic of *that* form of violence is the psychic numbing it requires, the dis-integration of the self, and its destruction of the community of mutual interaction.

We have seen that one characteristic of people who move away from that kind of violence is their ability to be moved. I have suggested that the central passion for non-violence is the ability of the self to be moved to accept suffering and even persecution for the sake of justice. Before it can become the true virtue of non-violence, however, this passion must be properly formed. That requires at least two features more: a proper anger, and the proper community. Both act to keep the passion for suffering from being destructive to the self.

As we read through the stories of the men in Everett's *Breaking Ranks*, we are struck by how often they acknowledge anger after their conversion. From the perspective of this book, I would say that they have discovered their anger. They had lost it because they were disintegrated in themselves (not attentive to their own embodiment), or because they were out of communion with the other (not attentive to

the interaction of the self and the other—especially in its physicality).
Thus we see that some of those who left said they just couldn't continue violating themselves, and some indicated an experience when they
were moved by considering the other. Their anger often turned then
toward the proper other: the structure that had disintegrated and dis-
connected them, and thus numbed and dehumanized them. The struggle also to have this anger in the right way, at the right time, etc., char-
acterizes all of them in their subsequent struggle for justice and peace.

Gandhi is well known for his statement that fighting—even with
physical force—is preferable to cowardice. In discussing that, he continues:

> But I believe nonviolence is infinitely superior to violence,
> forgiveness is more manly than punishment…. But…for-
> giveness only when there is the power to punish…. I there-
> fore appreciate the sentiment of those who cry out for the
> condign punishment of General Dyer [who executed the
> Amritsar massacre] and his ilk. They would tear him to
> pieces if they could.[21]

Here Gandhi indicates that non-violence is authentic only when it has
anger and the possibility of punishment as one of its features.[22] That is
because forgiveness is one of the essential dispositions for non-violence, and one cannot forgive until one acknowledges a wrong done to
the self. Non-violence is an activity of the strong, not a refuge for the
weak. Of course Gandhi means spiritual, not physical strength, as he
explains later in the same essay. In his attentiveness to anger, Gandhi
preserves the strength and dignity of the self threatened with violation.
Thus anger must be integrated (not done away with) to achieve the
virtue of non-violence.

I believe we can make the same point using the insights of
Thomas Aquinas to understand how we can integrate anger in our passion for justice. Thomas teaches that anger defends the self. But it is an
irascible passion. We have seen that he considers such passions to be
"between" passions—passions which begin and end in concupiscible
passions. The passion from which anger issues, and toward which it is
tending, is love. But the acceptance of suffering is not yet authentic
non-violence until it has first accomplished the journey of anger. The

love at the end of the journey of anger is different, of course, than the love at the beginning. That is because the love at the end does not cancel out, but embraces anger. It permeates, suffuses—or best, animates the anger. Carter Heyward is particularly insightful about this relationship throughout her work, *Our Passion for Justice*. She understands that "*love is justice*. Love does not come first, justice later," since

> our passion as lovers is what fuels both our rage at injustice—including that which is done to us—and our compassion, or our passion, which is on behalf of/in empathy with those who violate us and hurt us and would even destroy us.[23]

Attentiveness to the origin and goal (and especially, the final end) of anger is one thing which keeps our anger right. And I am saying here that the highest form of that love is found in the willingness to suffer. We must pay attention to the qualification "most immediately" when we say that the passion most immediately associated with justice is anger. For the cause of anger—and the ultimate purpose of justice—is love.

In fact, our love for the other is revealed precisely in our unwillingness to have the other persist in his injustice, since that is violative of the nature of the other. This explains why Stanley Hauerwas, in a recent discussion of peacemaking, states that "confrontation is at the heart of what it means to be a peacemaker."[24] In Tagalog, the words for non-violence are "alay dangal," which translate as "offer dignity to." The Filipinos sense that violence is a loss of dignity both for the victim and for the perpetrator. To offer a person a way out of doing violence is to offer to restore their dignity.[25]

It is Thomas' description of anger that begins and ends in love that would explain that "eagerness of lovers" that I sensed when the peace walkers at the Green Line prepared to encounter the military ranged against them. Though we ourselves were unarmed, there was a power and a strength there, and because we were non-violent I believe it was the power of God. In a private conversation with Coretta Scott King some years ago, I received this insight in another form. I questioned her about the time her house was bombed. After verifying the authenticity of Martin's commitment to non-violence during that incident, I pressed her for her own position. "But *you*," I said, "you're a mother. What would you have done if Yolanda *had* been killed? Would you have held to non-violence?" She replied, "It may sound strange to you now, but when you're in it—when you're in the movement—it's possible."

She meant, I believe, that she and Martin saw themselves as participating in a larger movement, a paradigmatic passion I would say, that was catching up even the structures of violence and death. Once, in a speech Martin King exhorted his listeners, if they were ever imprisoned for the sake of the movement, "to transform [that jail] from a dungeon of shame to a haven of human freedom and dignity." It seems that that is what Martin and Coretta Scott King, and all who practice the virtue of non-violence in pursuit of justice are doing: transforming the very structure of violence, in which so many are often numbingly locked, into a movement of non-violence, freedom and equality. In the end, then, we have enough practice in the virtue (the Latin root means "power") of non-violence to love even our enemies. That is because the power of non-violence is the power of God.

Audre Lorde begins one of her speeches by the blank and powerful statement, "My response to racism is anger."[26] As she elaborates on her passion, and if I understand her work correctly, we see that what angers her is that racism (and similar postures) *excludes* people and ruptures community. "Anger," she says, "is a grief of distortions between peers, and its object is change" (129). This leads us to reflect on a central theme of this book—that passions are constitutively interactive. To obscure or remove interaction is to obscure or remove passion. Put positively, our passion for justice must occur within a community.

The kind of society that is structured by hierarchical, competitive and exclusivistic notions of power cannot sustain the passions I have been writing about, and particularly not the passion for justice. Those with such passions, and particularly those with a passion for non-violence, will be marginalized, and even persecuted by such structures. But this ostracism turns out to be a privileged position for two reasons. First, one invariably finds a community on the margins, and that community practices, or is at least open to, the kinds of mutual interaction which are lacking in the dominant society.[27] Second, sufficient growth in the strength of the self in interaction with that community gives the self the virtue to turn and embrace the dominant society—even accepting its persecution—in the forgiving love that transforms. Thus Jerry Genesio founded Veterans for Peace, Gandhi founded his ashram, and Dorothy Day founded the Catholic Worker community. I believe that is why Jesus chose disciples and founded the church. As Hauerwas says, "The church does not have an alternative to war. The church is our alternative to war."[28]

Such communities of passion serve, by their inevitable interaction with the dominant society, to destabilize the rigid structures of that society and, in non-violent justice, to absorb and overcome them. Hauerwas writes, "[W]ithin a world of violence and injustice Christians can take the risk of being forgiven and forgiving. They are able to break the circle of violence as they refuse to become part of those institutions of fear that promise safety by the destruction of others."[29]

We find appreciation for the non-violent community especially in the works of Stanley Hauerwas. In *The Peaceable Kingdom*, for example, he writes, "...the kind of community in which we encounter another does not merely make *some* of the difference for our capacity for agency, it makes *all* the difference."[30] I support all that Hauerwas has written about community, but want to recall the expansion of the notion of agency which I offered in Chapter 2. With that added description of agent as "one who acts on behalf of another," we can see that the right kind of community will make us agents—missionaries of God's reign of justice and non-violence—to all. In Thomas' terms, the passion for God moves us to see the universal in every particular of our love; in Ignatius' terms, we would find God in *all* things. The right kind of community will allow the self ultimately to see the strength of its particularity precisely in its ability to love all—most especially those who would try to ostracize the self. It is the kind of community we were in Jamaica for Fabian, reaching out to his little brother.

In keeping with the themes presented in this book, I would say that the core of such a non-violent community would be a passion for, a companionship with, Jesus, who is presented to Christians as the incomparable Other, as our best friend, as God in the flesh. We have seen in the previous chapters that interaction with the other gradually transforms the self. So it is that by association with Jesus, in prayer and in community, we become in-formed with Jesus' own passion for God, and for God's reign of justice and peace. As Hauerwas says:

Thus to be like Jesus is to join him in the journey through which we are trained to be a people capable of claiming citizenship in God's kingdom of nonviolent love—a love that would overcome the powers of this world, not through coercion and force, but through the power of this one man's death.[31]

It is because we are more and more moved by Jesus *as embodied* that we increasingly become moved toward non-violence: more and more we come to see embodiment as sacred, and so become incapable of harming. John Howard Yoder tells a story of George Fox, advising William Penn in the forming of Pennsylvania as a non-violent state. At one point a delegation from the king of England came, and Penn, as governor, was to greet them formally. Part of his formal garb was a ceremonial sword. When Penn asked Fox whether it was acceptable to wear the sword, Fox is supposed to have responded, "Wear it as long as you can." The message is that the growth in virtue is accompanied by a concomitant growth in inability to do evil.[32] Ignatius has shown us how to associate with Jesus, how to be drawn by him in all our passions, and so to become like him. And that means that at a certain point, we simply cannot harm another human being;[33] we cannot even *wear* the sword. Tertullian says, "When he disarmed Peter, he disarmed every soldier."

From the perspective of one engaging in non-violent action, this cleansing of the whole self from violence through interaction with Jesus is important as well. It means that the anger and hatred directed toward the self cannot *resonate* within the self, cannot stir up corresponding violence within the self because we have become pure in heart. Instead, the power of God's non-violent love now permeates or suffuses, or, best, animates the self—even the embodied self—and absorbs and transforms the violence from the other. This purifying passion for God and for God's reign is why Jesus could recognize the action of God even in Pilate (Jn 19:11).

Finally, in his own body Jesus absorbed the violence of the religious and political structures of his day in his passion and cross, and transformed it in the resurrection through the power of the Spirit he shared with the Father. We call that transformation "forgiveness." Jesus spoke the words of forgiveness on the cross, and he breathed the

Spirit of forgiveness on the apostles after his resurrection. And it seems to me that the forgiveness and the resurrection power of the Spirit is concerned precisely with violence. That is, Jesus did not die a "natural" death. He was spat upon and crowned with thorns, shamed and scourged, stripped and crucified. He was killed by all the violence that the religious and political individuals and structures could invent and hurl against him. And when the Spirit raised Jesus from the dead, the Spirit raised him from *that* death—a death by violence. When the Spirit raised Jesus from the dead, it overcame, swallowed up, and transformed all the *violence* that individuals and structures could invent and employ, and presented the church with the transforming power of forgiveness.

The central virtue, then, toward which all Christians must learn to be drawn, is non-violence. For their part, Christians living in the Spirit cannot use the very violence which the Spirit of God has overcome. To do so would be to deny Jesus' resurrection from violence and to turn back to the works of death; it would be to violate the working of the resurrecting, forgiving and purifying Spirit in them and in the world; it would be, to quote Peter, like "a dog returning to its own vomit." Instead Christians become more and more non-violent as they more and more share in the Spirit that could raise Jesus even from death by violence. The Spirit creates that non-violent community which destabilizes "those institutions of fear that promise safety by the destruction of others," inviting them instead to become communities of mutuality, empowerment, and service. "Love your enemies, then, and pray for your persecutors, so that you may be children of your Father in heaven" (Mt 5:44).

Let us close this book as we began, with a reflection on Fabian, and his passions for his little brother who had been physically abused. We can recall that throughout the time of the school year, our community of prayer supported Fabian until he could overcome the effects of violence in his little brother's young life. In actuality, we formed a new community by reaching out to and embracing this young boy through Fabian, our agent. And all this was possible through the Spirit of Jesus in our prayer and in our midst. But it seems to me that the reign of God, the passion for justice, moves us even more radically. It moves us in the direction of a Dorothy Day or Gandhi, a Coretta Scott or Martin Luther King. It moves us to see our mission in the world as Ignatius saw it: as a struggle between the reign of God and the kingdom of Satan. If we refer to the story with which we opened this chapter, we see that it is almost impossible to imagine that we could convict such a young boy of enough "malice aforethought" to sustain the charge of murder of his friend. But the young boy partakes in a system (the evangelist John would call it "the world") that surely has enough violence structured into it to make such an act as the abusing, or even the shooting, of a child understandable. In our passion for justice, then, we are moved to challenge the very structures which require violence for their conservation, the structures which rupture communion among ourselves, which violate our integrity, which cause us to numb ourselves and in so many ways to obscure our paradigmatic passion—the passion for God. Of those many structures, such as racism, sexism, and economic classism, we have focused on militarism, which glories in the very violence that opposes the risen life of Jesus. And we overcome such structures not by force, since, as Ignatius of Antioch says, "force is no part of God."[34] We overcome them by the transforming suffering we have been considering in this chapter, by the non-violent Spirit of God poured out upon us as individuals, and as a community of faith. For as Thomas would tell us, freedom from compulsion by another is characteristic of the presence of the Spirit.

In Jesus, we see that Spirit evident in his passion for God, in his passion that God's reign of liberation, justice and compassion be accomplished on earth as it is in heaven, and finally in his passion, death and resurrection, into which Christians are baptized. And in joining that struggle for God's reign, we will ultimately find, in an echo of Dante's *Paradiso*, that his passion is our peace.

NOTES

Preface: Being Moved

1. See, for example, Plato (1963) *Republic* III.12, 401e-402a, and *Laws* II.653a-654d.
2. All references to Aristotle will be from Aristotle's *Nicomachean Ethics,* trans. by Martin Ostwald (NY: The Bobbs-Merrill Co., Inc., 1962), unless otherwise noted.
3. Cf. 1115b15-20. My translation of the Greek πάθος and its forms is "passion," not "emotion," as in Ostwald. I believe that translation more clearly brings out the distinction Aristotle intends, especially in passages like the one quoted.
4. 1104b15. Cf. 1104b28-29; 1105a10-17.
5. Paul J. Wadell, C.P., *Friendship and the Moral Life* (Notre Dame: University of Notre Dame Press, 1989), p. 15.
6. Researcher Klaus Scherer, for example, reports that there have been "several attempts to produce comprehensive lists of emotion related labels," yielding over five hundred English terms and over two hundred German terms. "On the Nature and Function of Emotion: A Component Process Approach," *Approaches to Emotion,* eds. Klaus R. Scherer and Paul Ekman (Hillsdale: Lawrence Erlbaum Associates, Inc., 1984), p. 297.
7. The need for such a project may be seen from reading Alisdair MacIntyre, *After Virtue* (Notre Dame: University of Notre Dame Press, 1981). MacIntyre's thesis is that the confusion of contempo-

rary ethical discourse occurs because each position is a shard of a fragmented whole, inhabiting a different narrative, so that true dialogue is impossible. Such confusion is inevitable, since contemporary ethicists have lost touch with their ancestry (see especially p. 53). Barry Arnold presents an analysis and direct reconstructive reply to that thesis in *The Pursuit of Virtue: The Union of Moral Psychology and Ethics*. American University Studies. Series V: Philosophy, Vol. 65 (New York: Peter Lang, 1989).

1. The Body

1. In the Hippocratic model, the passions were caused by humors; in the Galenic model, by the movements of the vascular system. See Karl Pribram, "Emotion: A Neurobehavioral Analysis," *Approaches to Emotion,* pp. 14ff.
2. Martin Kemp, ed., *Leonardo on Painting: An Anthology of Writings by Leonardo da Vinci with a Selection of Documents Relating to His Career as an Artist.* Selectors, trans., Martin Kemp and Margaret Walker (New Haven and London: Yale University Press, 1989), p. 146. The literature in this area is quite extensive. See, for example, the work of Anthony Blunt on Nicolas Poussin or Julius S. Held and Donald Posner on Charles LeBrun.
3. John R. Gillis, "From Ritual to Romance: Toward an Alternative History of Love," *Emotion and Social Change: Toward a New Psychohistory,* eds. Carol Z. Stearns and Peter N. Stearns (New York: Holmes & Meier, 1988), p. 4.
4. "Ego cogito, ergo sum," *Principia philosophiae,* Vol. 8, *Oeuvres de Descartes,* publieés par Charles Adam et Paul Tannery (Paris: Librairie Philosophique J. Vrin [1644] 1964), I.vii.8. The *Discours de la Méthod, Oeuvres* ([1637] 1965), presented "Je pense donc je suis" to the French-speaking public (IV.33.19).
5. See Jack Rochford Vrooman, *René Descartes, an Autobiography* (New York: Putnam, 1970), for the effect of Descartes' historical *environ* on his philosophy.
6. "Les passions de l'âme," Vol. 11, *Oeuvres de Descartes,* ([1645-6] 1967), pp. 327-488. Actually, Descartes has the soul itself seated in "a little gland which lies in the middle of the brain" (art. xxxiv).

This gland (and, with it, the soul), is pushed one way or the other by "spirits" which either emanate from the mind (or sometimes the soul itself), or by "animal spirits" which intrude from outside.

7. Joseph Heller, *Something Happened* (New York: Alfred Knopf, 1974), p. 569.

8. It is interesting to note that Solomon, at the conclusion of his study of romantic love, offers "excitement" as a virtue. "The Virtue of Love," *Midwest Studies in Philosophy* (Notre Dame: University of Notre Dame Press, 1988), pp. 12-31.

9. *Religion within the Limits of Reason Alone,* tr. by Th. M. Greene and H.H. Hudson (New York: Harper Torchbooks [1793] 1960), p. 85.

10. See, for example, James Hillman, *Emotion, a Comprehensive Phenomenology of Theories and the Meanings for Therapy* (London: Routledge & Kegan Paul, 1960) or Warren Shibles, *Emotion* (Whiteware: The Language Press, The University of Wisconsin, 1974). Still the best general historical overview in English of theories of emotion, though dated, is H.M. Gardiner, R.C. Metcalf, and John G. Beebe-Center, *Feeling and Emotion: A History of Theories* (Westport: Greenwood Press [1937] 1970). For an excellent brief historical overview, see Susan J. Bandy, "A Humanistic Interpretation of the Mind-Body Problem in Western Thought," in *Mind and Body: East Meets West,* Seymour Kleinman, ed. (Champaign: Human Kinetics Publishers, 1986), pp. 25-30. For a good summary contemporary scientific study on the passions, see K.T. Strongman, *The Psychology of Emotion,* 3rd ed. (New York: John Wiley & Sons, 1987), ch. 2.

11. Even in 1988, Solomon can write, "Indeed, we might even say that the 'truth' of emotions is their intractability, their resistance to every attempt to change them." "The Virtue of Love," p. 19.

12. Thus Kant, in triumph or frustration, called the passions "the sicknesses of the character." *Anthropologie im pragmatischer Hinsicht* (Königsberg: Friedrich Nicolovius), sec. 71. Even though David Hume tried to recover the importance of passions by writing "[R]eason is, and ought only to be, the slave of the passions, and can never pretend to any other office than to serve and obey them," we can still see the false dichotomy between reason and passion in his presuppositions. David Hume, "On the Passions,"

Treatise on Human Nature, in *The Philosophical Works of David Hume*, Vol. 2 (Boston: Little, Brown and Company, [1757], 1854), II.iii.3, p. 166; Cf. III.i.1, pp. 218ff.

13. For the grammar of "disturbance," see, for example, R.S. Peters, *The Education of the Emotions* (London: Allen & Unwin, 1970), p. 4 and *passim*.

14. Charles Darwin, "The Expression of Emotion in Man and Animals," *What is an Emotion? Classic Readings in Philosophical Psychology,* eds. Cheshire Calhoun and Robert C. Solomon (New York and Oxford: Oxford University Press, 1984), p. 123.

15. Robert Plutchik, "Emotions: A General Psychoevolutionary Theory," *Approaches to Emotion*, p. 197.

16. Arthur Peacocke, *God and the New Biology* (San Francisco: Harper and Row, 1987). Humans used to think of themselves as the only subjects, Peacocke argues, and everything else as objects; "to regard their surroundings as a kind of stage on which their own personal drama is enacted, themselves in the foreground" (120). But evolutionary science has changed that, giving us a sense of commonality (122).

17. I have used the word "modern" to refer to treatments beginning with Descartes, and the word "contemporary" to refer to those treatments beginning with William James' "What is an Emotion?" which appeared in *Mind* in 1884 because "it continues to be the starting-point for most contemporary theories of emotion, however they may disagree on its initial formulation." Cheshire Calhoun and Robert C. Solomon, *What is an Emotion?* p. 126.

18. James, "What is an Emotion?" *What is an Emotion?* p. 128.

19. Aquinas also believed this. James also held that "a necessary corollary of [my theory] ought to be that any voluntary arousal of the so called manifestations of a special emotion ought to give us the emotion itself" (136).

20. Later, however, "James (1894) himself rejected Lange's view that cardiovascular changes were the central cause of emotional states and argued that any sympathetic or somatic response may trigger emotional states." Jack George Thompson, "The Psychobiology of Emotions," *Emotions, Personality, and Psychotherapy*, gen. eds. Carroll E. Izard and Jerome L. Singer (New York and London: Plenum Press, 1988), p. 267.

21. Cannon also demonstrated that animals with the brain severed from the nervous system still retained emotional behavior, and that different emotions evinced similar visceral behavior. "Bodily Changes in Pain, Hunger, Fear and Rage: A Critical Examination of the James-Lange Theory of Emotions," *What is an Emotion?* pp. 143-151.

22. For experimental evidence that the entire brain is involved in affectivity, see, for example, Pavel V. Simonov, "The Information Theory of Emotion," *Feelings and Emotions: The Loyola Symposium,* ed. Magda Arnold (New York and London: The Academic Press, 1970), pp. 145-149, and Antonio R. Damasio, and G.W. Van Hoesen, "Emotional Disturbance Associated with Focal Lesions of the Limbic Frontal Lobe," *Neuropsychology of Human Emotion. Advances in Neuropsychology and Behavioral Neurology,* eds. Kenneth M. Heilman and Paul Satz (New York, London: The Guilford Press, 1983), pp. 85-110.

23. "Feelings as Monitors," in *The Loyola Symposium,* pp. 41-54; *Languages of the Brain* (Englewood Cliffs: Prentice-Hall, 1971), pp. 41-54; "Emotion: A Neurobehavioral Analysis," *Approaches to Emotion,* pp. 13-38.

24. Charles Hampden-Turner, *Maps of the Mind* (New York: Macmillan, 1981), p. 94.

25. Emotion would then be a "felt dishabituation" in response to "incongruous input." "Emotion: A Neurobehavioral Analysis," p. 21.

26. For further experiments with this phenomenon, see Alan Gevins, et al., "Human Neuroelectric Patterns Predict Performance Accuracy," *Science* 1987, Vol. 235, pp. 580-584.

27. We can perhaps also begin to understand why a particular physical demeanor gives evidence of *virtue* to Aristotle, *NE* 1125a13-17.

28. See, for example, "A person is not a mind 'in' a Body: he is a self-identifying temporal unity-continuity whose qualiative [sic] lived-body mediates what is the Body and the Environment with which he interacts." In Peter A. Bertocci, *The Person and Primary Emotions: Recent Research in Psychology* (New York and Berlin: Springer-Verlag, 1988), p. 87. Also cf. Silvan Tomkins, "Affect as the Primary Motivational System," *The Loyola Symposium,* pp. 101-110; "Affect Theory," *Approaches to Emotion,* pp. 163-195,

and R.B. Zajonc, "The Interaction of Affect and Cognition," *Approaches to Emotion*, pp. 239-246; "On Primacy of Affect," *Approaches to Emotion*, pp. 259-70.

29. For interesting examples of "avoidance conditioning," and the inability of certain forms of aversive measures to overcome the genetic "nature," see Melvin Konner, *The Tangled Wing: Biological Constraints on the Human Spirit* (New York: Holt, Rinehart and Winston, 1982), pp. 26-27.

30. Pribram's (1984) definition of emotion as a "felt dishabituation" in response to "incongruous input" (21) does not allow for passions of joy or delight that would come from a more constant interaction with a beloved other. Peter Bertocci tries to distinguish between "my lived-body" and "my pencil," "mainly by the degree of causal control I can exert over each." *The Person and Primary Emotions: Recent Research in Psychology*, p. 87.

31. Paul Ekman, "Biological and Cultural Contributions to Body and Facial Movement in the Expression of Emotions," *Explaining Emotions,* ed. Amélie Rorty (Berkeley: University of California Press, 1980), pp. 73-102; "Expression and the Nature of Emotion," *Approaches to Emotion,* pp. 319-343.

32. "Biological and Cultural Contributions to Body and Facial Movement in the Expression of Emotions," p. 97. *Experiencing Emotion: A Cross-cultural Study,* eds. Klaus R. Scherer, Harald G. Wallbott, and Angela B. Summerfield (Cambridge: Cambridge University Press, 1986), is devoted entirely to cross-cultural studies of affectivity. Harald G. Wallbott and Klaus R. Scherer have concluded from their research that there is cross-cultural agreement even on the morality or propriety of certain affective states such as disgust, anger, fear or joy, with joy predictably "considered more moral than other emotions." In "How Universal and Specific is Emotional Experience? Evidence from 27 Countries on Five Continents," *Facets of Emotion, Recent Research,* ed. Klaus R. Scherer (Hillsdale: Lawrence Erlbaum Associates, Inc., 1988), p. 54.

33. Ekman's findings thus support both James-Lange and Aquinas. What is unique is that Ekman asked his subjects not to "act/look frightened" (which invariably led other researchers to failure) but

to assume minutely recorded demeanors of facial musculature he had recorded as characteristic of angry or frightened people.

34. Nico H. Frijda, *The Emotions* (Cambridge: Cambridge University Press, 1986), pp. 126ff.

35. This includes blood pressure and blood flow distribution, vasodilatation and vasoconstriction. Frijda also notes that "under most conditions, blood pressure rapidly returns to base level after the emotional events have terminated. However, intense and prolonged emotional stress can lead to level increases that far outlast stimulation and eventually lead to tonically increased levels of indefinite duration" (130).

36. Skin conductivity (SC) and electrodermal response (EDR) are both measures of the skin's electrical conductance. EDR is phasic (lasting a short time), and SC is tonic (lasting longer periods).

37. Cf. also Neil McNaughton, *Biology and Emotion,* Vol. 5 of *Problems in the Behavioural Sciences*, gen. ed. Jeffrey Gray (Cambridge, New York, and Melbourne: Cambridge University Press, 1989), pp. 57ff, for emotion-specific releases of hormones.

38. Cf. Ekman, "Expression and the Nature of Emotion," p. 326: "...the ANS activity differed not just between positive and negative emotions, but also...there were different patterns of ANS changes for anger versus disgust, and either anger or distrust as compared to fear or surprise." Also see Wallbott and Scherer, "How Universal and Specific is Emotional Experience," p. 35: "For physiological symptoms, we would expect skin temperature sensations to differentiate the four emotions strongly, with joy being experienced as 'warm,' anger as 'hot,' and sadness and fear as 'cold.'"

39. Melvin Konner has demonstrated that enriched environment for laboratory rats actually stamped physically observable differences in the brain. *The Tangled Wing*, p. 61.

40. Gerald G. May, *Addiction and Grace* (San Francisco: Harper and Row, 1988), gives us a fascinating account of the physiological changes accruing from substance and non-substance attachments (pp. 75-90).

41. He distinguishes the true facial expression (called the "elicitor") from culturally determined "display rules," in "Biological and

Cultural Contributions to Body and Facial Movement in the Expression of Emotions," pp. 80, 95.

42. "Expression and the Nature of Emotion," p. 326.

43. Douglas Hofstadter, *Metamagical Themas: Questing for the Essence of Mind and Pattern* (Camp Hill: Basic Books, 1984), p. 236.

44. Thus Frijda, *The Emotions,* pp. 455-456, proposes that for a good model of affectivity, we need an analyzer, comparator, diagnoser, evaluator, action proposer, physiological change generator, and actor.

45. Klaus Scherer proposes a progressive sequence of stimulus evaluation checks (SEC), but then has trouble accounting for emotive "responses" with "minimal cognition." "On the Nature and Function of Emotion: A Component Process Approach," *Approaches to Emotion,* p. 306. Cf. also Robert Plutchik, "Emotions: A General Psychoevolutionary Theory," *Approaches to Emotion,* pp. 197-219.

46. It seems that the destruction takes place when we approach what we should avoid, or avoid what we should approach. I hope in a future book to discuss the relationship between the classical category of "vice" and the modern notion of "addiction."

47. "On the Nature and Function of Emotion," p. 295.

48. Richard Lazarus, "Thoughts on the Relation between Emotion and Cognition," *Approaches to Emotion,* p. 249. Cf. Silvan S. Tomkins (1984), "The generality of time, object, intensity and density of the affect system are not the *consequence* of learning but rather the structural, innate features of the affect system that make learning possible" (166). Cf. R.B. Zajonc, "On Primacy of Affect," *Approaches to Emotion,* pp. 259-270 for research that, in the case of language perception, "semantic features of words are accessible *earlier than* perceptions of physical stimulus" (265-266, emphasis added). Cf. also Gevins, et al., "Human Neuroelectric Patterns" for the theory of "preparatory patterns."

49. *Metamagical Themas,* p. 652. Those familiar with the field theory of Kurt Lewin will see similarities here.

50. The German word for disposition is *Bestimmung,* which has its etymological roots in the notion of "attunement." For a commentary on this feature of affectivity, see Francis Dunlop, *The Education of Feeling and Emotion* (London: Allen & Unwin, 1984), p. 47.

51. J.P. Scott, "The Function of Emotions in Behavioural Systems: A Systems Theory Analysis," *Theories of Emotion,* eds. R. Plutchik and H. Kellerman, Vol. 1 of *Emotion: Theory, Research and Experience* (New York: Academic Press, 1980), pp. 33-56.

52. H.F. Harlow and M.K. Harlow, "Social deprivation in monkeys," *Scientific American,* 1962, Vol. 207, pp. 136-46, and Neil McNaughton, *Biology and Emotion,* pp. 99-100. Though the results are illuminating, I must confess to a sadness and discomfort at the long-term deprivation of the young monkeys.

53. Neil McNaughton, *Biology and Emotion,* pp. 130-131.

54. Cf., for example, K.T. Strongman, *The Psychology of Emotion,* p. 167, and the social psychologist Norman K. Denzin, *On Understanding Emotions* (San Francisco: Jossey-Bass, 1984), p. 50.

55. "The Organization of Emotional Development," *Approaches to Emotion,* pp. 109-128.

56. Colwyn Trevarthen, "Emotions in Infancy: Regulators of Contact and Relationships with Persons," *Approaches to Emotion,* p. 136.

57. See the excellent study by Elaine Hatfield, John T. Cacioppo, Richard Rapson, "The Logic of Emotion: Emotional Contagion," *Review of Personality and Social Psychology* [in press, 1992].

2. Philosophical and Theological Approaches to the Passions

1. William C. Spohn, S.J., "Notes on Moral Theology: 1990, Passions and Principles," *Theological Studies,* Vol. 52, No. 1 (March 1991), p. 69.

2. J.R.S. Wilson, *Emotion and Object* (Cambridge: Cambridge University Press, 1972). Cf. p. 3.

3. W.D. Hart, *The Engines of the Soul* (Cambridge and New York: Cambridge University Press, 1988).

4. Note that in concluding his work "On Being Affected," G.D. Marshall calls affection "a disturbance which we can either give expression to or try to master" (*Mind,* 1968, Vol. 77, p. 259).

5. W.D. Hart, *Engines of the Soul,* p. 30, emphasis added; cf. pp. 69ff.

6. Wilson, *Emotion and Object,* p. 178. See also Norman Dent, *The Moral Psychology of the Virtues* (Cambridge: Cambridge University Press, 1984), p. 82: "Most fundamentally, it [love, which Dent calls 'the basic source of all passions'] is the investing of concern or care in something as being something of importance, value or good to one in one way or another"; and Marshall, "On Being Affected," writes that the object of our affection "is what we have evaluatively classified or regarded in such a way that the affection flows or persists" (245).

7. See also Wilson, *Emotion and Object,* pp. 37ff, for a similar discussion.

8. Dunlop's most powerful contribution is the linking together of "bios" passions (i.e. for food, warmth, etc.) with the "higher passions" for self-transcendence. But Dunlop seems to imply a definite "break" in the development from the needs of "bios," to the "higher values," a break characterized by the necessity to "tear oneself away from oneself." Francis Dunlop, *The Education of Feeling and Emotion* (London: Allen & Unwin, 1984), p. 47.

9. See also Marshall, "On Being Affected," "Being affected restricts the range of considerations open to one's judgement, and so reliable judgement is difficult.... And sometimes our faculty of judgement is entirely impaired" (246). Marshall never gives a favorable portrayal of the passions in this work.

10. Magda Arnold, *Emotion and Personality* (New York: Columbia University Press, 1960), Vol. I, p. 182. In "Cognition and Feeling," *Feelings and Emotions: The Loyola Symposium,* Magda Arnold, ed. (New York and London: The Academic Press, 1970), p. 176, the Cognitivist Silvano Arieti adopts Arnold's definition of emotion in its entirety. The Cognitivist James Averill states that "every emotional reaction is a function of a particular kind of appraisal," so that "one of the major problems for the study of emotions is thus the elucidation of the appraisals on which the various emotions are based." "Emotion and Anxiety: Sociocultural, Biological and Psychological Determinants," *Explaining Emotions,* p. 64.

11. "Perennial Problems in the Field of Emotion," *The Loyola Symposium,* p. 182, emphasis added.

12. Magda Arnold, *Memory and the Brain* (Hillsdale: Lawrence Erlbaum Associates, 1984), p. 23 (emphasis added).

13. Philosophers quickly move to a strong (intellective and deliberative) sense of "appraisal" when they discuss the role of the intellect in affectivity, though such a move finds insufficient warrant from contemporary scientific research. Calhoun is alert to that equivocation in "Cognitive Emotions?" *What is an Emotion?* p. 341.

    In *The Passions* (Garden City: Anchor Press, Doubleday, 1976), Robert Solomon ends by collapsing the intellective and the affective states (judgment and reason). He writes, for example, "On our account, anger is not a feeling, nor does it involve any identifiable feeling" (p. 255, cf. 254, 276). Thus his claim that "emotion is a judgment" seems more of a tautology than an insight.

14. For a typically illuminating discussion of this phenomenon, see Stanley Hauerwas' consideration of the case of Olin Teague, in the chapter "Reconciling the Practice of Reason," *Christian Existence Today, Essays on Church, World and Living In Between* (Durham: The Labyrinth Press, 1988), pp. 67-87.

15. Michael Stocker, "Intellectual Desire, Emotion, and Action," in *Explaining*, pp. 323-338, also attempts to acknowledge the organic dimension of affectivity and sets out expressly to rectify the Cartesian view (p. 323). But his project applies more to emotions than passions and tries to model emotional activity too much on that of the intellect, cf. p. 326.

16. Amélie Rorty, *Mind in Action: Essays in the Philosophy of Mind* (Boston: Beacon Press, 1988), p. 101.

17. Amélie Rorty, "Explaining Emotions," in *Explaining Emotions*, pp. 107ff.

18. "The Historicity of Psychological Attitudes," *Mind in Action,* pp. 121-134.

19. That is a systemic difficulty for Rorty. We see that in "Explaining Emotions," she gives us no criteria by which people can judge what might be inappropriate or irrational about their passions, and no effective "purchase point" from which the habit can be changed. If by another habit, then which one? If by "secondary

emotions," how can a secondary emotion rehabituate a primary one?

20. Sarah Conly, "Flourishing and the Ethics of Virtue," *Midwest Studies in Philosophy,* pp. 92-94.

21. Don Saliers, *The Soul in Paraphrase, Prayer and the Religious Affections* (New York: Seabury, 1980), p. 11. In that he expressly follows Jonathan Edwards, whom he quotes as saying: "True religion consists in the practical exercise of the will, where the deeper affections are 'motives and wellsprings' of desire and action" (p. 9). See also Andrew J. Burgess, *Passion, "Knowing How" and Understanding: An Essay on the Concept of Faith* (Missoula: The Scholars Press, 1975), p. 2: "How far and in what ways is the sharing of a distinctive mode of passions a prerequisite for learning the Christian truth?" This question is similar to the one we will see in James M. Gustafson, *Can Ethics Be Christian?* (Chicago: University of Chicago Press, 1975). Hereafter cited as Gustafson, 1975.

22. *Ibid.*, p. 7. Saliers chooses the word "affections" because it is not as theory-laden and as broad as emotion, and because he is drawing upon the work of Jonathan Edwards.

23. Robert Roberts, *Spirituality and Human Emotions* (Grand Rapids: Eerdmans, 1982), begins by speaking of what seems to be a continuum of human passions: "We all have a pre-reflective, animal-like hope which needs to be educated into the solid emotion of eternal hope" (p. 1).

    What seems to be lacking, though, is precisely that interrelational quality such that we could understand such emotions as shared by God in prayer. In the end, then, we are humble if we regard all others as equal (58), but not because we have the vision of Christ humble; we are grateful because we "assent to belief in salvation by Christ" (78), but not because we have come to partake in the thanksgiving prayers of Christ himself.

24. Saliers does say, "The question is not 'To what does prayer respond?' but 'To Whom?'" But he immediately follows with, "Christian prayer responds to *a world* known most fully in and through the judgement and mercy of God in Jesus Christ" (p. 95, emphasis added). He does say, "Those who pray with [Christ] are participants in his relationship to God the Father—the relationship

of love and self-giving which is the Holy Spirit" (p. 47), but Saliers does not work that out in his own discussion.

25. Consideration of the reality of Christian community would help Burgess in his project as well. The difficulty in his work is that he makes too great a dichotomy between the "how" and the "what" of faith. For an excellent study of the importance of the right *content* in faith, see Stanley Hauerwas, "On Taking Religion Seriously: The Challenge of Jonestown," *Against the Nations, War and Survival in a Liberal Society* (San Francisco: Harper & Row, 1988), pp. 91-106.

Evans makes a similar mistake in *Struggle and Fulfillment* (Philadelphia: Fortress Press, 1981) when he holds that "[propositional] beliefs are actually secondary" (p. 12). Eventually they become so "secondary" to the primacy of the basic pre-linguistic experience that they are essentially irrelevant. I recommend the incisive analysis of this problem in Paul Lauritzen's dissertation, *Religious Belief and Emotions: The Moral Transformation of the Self* (Brown, 1985), pp. 51-60.

26. Gustafson, 1975, p. 65.

27. "[They] are 'habits' in the classical Roman Catholic usage of that term...persisting tendencies to act in such a way that one's action is directed in part by lasting dispositions." James M. Gustafson, *Christ and the Moral Life* (New York: Harper & Row, 1968), p. 248. Hereafter cited as Gustafson, 1968. Cf. also Gustafson, 1975, p. 40, and p. 45, where he refers to dispositions as the "conditions for the possibility of acting."

28. "Character comes into visibility only through actions, and thus we see its effects when persons respond to other persons or to events in a manner that has some consistency with their actions under similar conditions." James M. Gustafson, *Christian Ethics and the Community* (Philadelphia: Pilgrim Press, 1971), p. 170. Hereafter cited as Gustafson, 1971. He more colloquially calls character "the sort of person one is," in Gustafson, 1975, p. 9 and *passim.*

29. Gustafson, 1971, p. 180. In answer to the question: "Are there common Christian characteristics of life that form a class of behavior or of persons?" on p. 178.

30. Cf. especially Gustafson, 1975, p. 47.

31. Pp. 98-106. Neither does he mention the passions in his later stud-

ies of Aquinas, as for example in *Ethics from a Theocentric Perspective* (Chicago: The University of Chicago Press, 1984), Vol. 2, pp. 42-64, though he suggests that Thomistic reflection might benefit from a notion of interdependence with nature (p. 57).

32. See Richard A. McCormick, "Gustafson's God: Who? What? Where? (Etc.)," *The Journal of Religious Ethics* Vol. 13, No. 1 (Spring 1985), pp. 53-70, especially p. 58 for the question of Gustafson's Christology.

33. The most complete treatment of the inadequacy of Gustafson's Christological claims is found in Brian Linnane, *Rahnerian Christology as an Anthropological Foundation for a Theocentric Ethic* [Yale Dissertation: in press].

34. Arthur C. McGill, *Suffering, A Test of Theological Method* (Philadelphia: Westminster Press, 1982, 1st pub. 1968), p. 73.

35. *Ibid.*, pp. 76, 78. I want to claim that same Trinitarian understanding of God as the systematic undergirding for my "interactive model" of the passions as "constitutively interrelational," "experiences of empowerment," or, as McGill would say, as "mutual self-giving," since theological reflection on the significance of Christ and of his suffering propelled the Christian faith toward a distinctively Trinitarian understanding of God.

36. I simply cannot recall if this insight is original. If a reader can find a reference, I would be grateful.

37. Patricia Jung, in "Sanctification: An Interpretation in Light of Embodiment," *Journal of Religious Ethics* Vol. 11, No. 1 (Spring 1983), criticizes Hauerwas for ignoring the passions and "the ancestral roots of action which arise involuntarily from the body," in his account of character (p. 78). Hauerwas takes account of Jung's earlier dissertation critique in Stanley Hauerwas, *A Community of Character* (Notre Dame: University of Notre Dame Press, 1981), p. 267, n. 55 (hereafter cited as Hauerwas, *Community*), admitting "there is a great deal that is right about this criticism."

38. Stanley Hauerwas, *Character and the Christian Life* (San Antonio: Trinity University Press, 1975), p. 96. Hereafter cited as *Character*. And, "the moral task consists in acquiring the skills,

i.e., the character, which enable us to negotiate the many kinds and levels of narrative in a truthful manner." *Community,* p. 11.

39. He continues, "To have Christian character is to have our 'seeing' of the world directed by the fundamental symbols of the language of faith." *Character,* p. 203. See also *Vision and Virtue* (Notre Dame: Fides/Claretian, 1974) (hereafter cited as *Vision*), p. 67, and *Christian Existence Today*, "The Gesture of a Truthful Story," pp. 101-110.

40. *Character,* p. 203 (emphasis added).

41. *Character,* p. 107. See Gilbert Ryle, "The Concept of Mind," in *What is an Emotion?* p. 260 for a similar question and insight on character.

42. *Character,* p. 106. Hauerwas has captured the significance of assumption of bodily demeanors, or "practices," in all his work.

43. But he immediately adds, "*Character,* of course, is not a theoretical notion, but merely the name we give to the cumulative source of human *actions.*" Stanley Hauerwas, *Truthfulness and Tragedy* (Notre Dame: University of Notre Dame, 1977), p. 29 (second emphasis added). Also, "Much of what we are is that which 'happens to us.' As I tried to indicate in my discussion of intentionality, the passive resides at the very core of our agency, for our intentions embody the passive elements of our existence as elements in the envisaged project." *Character,* p. 116.

44. *Character,* p. 112. See also, "To be free is the successful embodiment of the descriptions we choose as morally true." *Vision,* p. 65, or "... our task, through the power of practical reason, is to change the way things are by changing ourselves." *Christian Existence Today,* p. 74. Oftentimes reading such quotes one finds it difficult to dissuade oneself that Hauerwas' final "court of appeal" is the individual's choice after all.

45. *Community,* p. 147. Hauerwas presents us with a fascinating personal account of "regret" there, and its importance for the notion of "agency."

46. Julian Hartt, *A Christian Critique of American Culture* (New York: Harper & Row, 1967), p. 198, quoted from *Community,* p. 235, n. 43. Again, Hauerwas does not follow up on this full notion of agency.

47. *Community,* p. 130.

3. Overview of the Theology of Thomas Aquinas

1. I am using St. Thomas Aquinas, *Summa Theologiae* (Blackfriars, 1964), the Blackfriars text and their notation system for the *Summa theologiae*. I will cite each translator-commentator as necessary in the discussion.

2. There are many, but perhaps the best is James A. Weisheipl, *Friar Thomas D'Aquino, His Life, Thought and Works* (Washington, D.C.: Catholic University Press, 1983).

3. Such scholars as Ya'cub ibn Ishaq al-Kindi (c. 801-66), al-Farabi (d. 950), and al-Husayn ibn 'Abdullah ibn Sina (Avicenna) (980-1037).

4. In Andalus, Muhammad ibn Ahmad ibn Rushd (Averroes) (1126-98), wrote over two hundred and fifty treatises, many of them on Aristotle. Much of this history is taken from Albert Hourani, *A History of the Arab Peoples* (Cambridge: The Belknap Press of Harvard University Press, 1991), pp. 74-79, 174ff. See also Alasdair MacIntyre, *Whose Justice? Which Rationality?* (Notre Dame: University of Notre Dame Press, 1988), pp. 164-168.

5. It is interesting to note that many Muslims had the same difficulty reconciling Aristotle, and philosophy in general, with the faith of their scripture, *Qur'an*, as did the Christians.

6. Cf. Amin Maalouf, *The Crusades Through Arab Eyes* (New York: Schocken Press, 1987).

7. The best for understanding the intellectual background and project is Alasdair MacIntyre, *Whose Justice? Which Rationality?* pp. 164-207.

8. Translation of Ibn Rushd's *Fasl al-maqal (Averroes on the Harmony of Religion and Philosophy),* by Albert Hourani, quoted in his *History,* pp. 174-175.

9. However, about two dozen of his theological propositions were condemned by the bishop of Paris in 1277. On August 4, 1879, Pope Leo XIII wrote the encyclical "Aeterni Patris," which encouraged study and interest in Thomas and promoted a rebirth in Thomistic studies.

10. For the best discussion of the ideas of this and the next paragraph, see David Burrell, *Exercises in Religious Understanding* (Notre Dame: University of Notre Dame Press, 1974), ch. 3, and *Aquinas,*

God and Action (London: Routledge and Kegan Paul, 1975), especially pp. 14-18. Of course, we can say that we know that God is.

11. Cf. the *Summa,* I.5.1, and I.16.3.

12. The formal cause of the rock, or its "rockness," is due to the secondary causes that produced the rock.

13. Lawrence Dewan, "The Real Distinction between Intellect and Will," *Angelicum,* Vol. 57 (1980), p. 584. Dewan presents the point of his article in the title. Here he accurately portrays the two distinct perfectibilities of things, but in his discussion, particularly of sensate beings, he more carefully indicates the interrelation between the two perfectibilities.

14. Eric D'Arcy presents this point very well in his Introduction to I-II, 22-30, Vol. 19, p. xxiv (Blackfriars).

15. We would have to refine our understanding of Thomas before we claimed complete agreement with Darwin. Thomas does not believe that good and evil are of equal power. Therefore approach is a much more powerful dynamic than avoidance; avoidance is almost a logical consequence of approach in Thomas.

16. Richard R. Baker points out that in Thomas' discussion of "nature," the distinction between "nature" and "the orectic power [*appetitus*]" is not a real, but a virtual distinction. *The Thomistic Theory of the Passions and their Influence upon the Will* (Notre Dame: University of Notre Dame Press, 1941), p. 14. Cf. Thomas' *Commentary on the Nicomachean Ethics,* III, 13, and also *Summa* I-II.8.a1.

17. That human beings give birth to other human beings is also a matter of natural order for Thomas.

18. Cf. I-II.24.4 and 26.1 for Thomas' discussion of this.

19. I took this excellent example of a cat stalking a bird from G.E.M. Anscombe, *Intention* (Oxford: Basil Blackwell, 1958), pp. 85-86. She writes, "Thus the possession of sensible discrimination and that of volition are inseparable; one cannot describe a creature as having the power of sensation without also describing it as doing things in accordance with perceived sensible differences" (p. 67). Also cf. *Summa,* I-II.40.3.

20. *Quaes. Disp. De Ver.* 22.4.

21. *Ibid.*

22. See I.80.2. Cf. also Aristotle's *De Anima*, III.10, 433b16; and his *Metaphysics*, XI.7, 1072a26.

23. "Intellectual operations supervene on those of a sensory nature." John Patrick Reid, translator and commentator, Vol. 21, Appendix VII, p. 182.

24. See I.80.1.

25. Cf. *Summa contra gentiles*, II.81. Rational beings participate in divine reason in a more excellent way, "in that they participate in providence, providing for themselves and for others" (I-II.91.3).

26. *In I Ad Cor. XV*, lect. 2. Cf. also *Summa*, I.76.8, and I.75.2.ad3. That insistence actually gets Thomas into a little intellectual trouble earlier in the *Summa*. Thomas, because of his insistence on the unity of the soul and body, simply cannot figure out how the soul in heaven (before the general resurrection for the body) could know anything without its bodily senses to inform it. He finally settles on the theory that God will give knowledge to the soul by "a kind of light." Cf. I.75.6, and I.89.1.

    My colleague Dr. James Long points out that Thomas' view of the human composite does give urgency to, and provides a rationale for, the revealed doctrine of the resurrection of the body.

27. "[N]o human action is predicated of the soul, as though it were the ultimate subject of predication, and this applies even to the highest acts of mind and will...man needs body and bodily organs in all that he does, thinks and wills." Albert Regan, "Human Body in Moral Theology. Some Basic Orientations," *Studia Moralia,* Vol. 17 (1979), p. 173. Cf. also Abelardo Lobato, "El principio libertad. El dinamismo orignario de la voluntad en la cuestión VI *De Malo* de Sant Tommasso de Aquino," *Doctor Communis* Vol. 50 (1977), p. 54.

28. Aquinas will say, for example, that the passions are disposed to obey the governance of the intellect, in I-II.50.3.ad1.

29. We can also use the distinction between substantial and accidental perfection here. The human being is already (substantially) perfect and not-yet (accidentally) perfect.

30. "Man not merely recognizes, and strives for, the particulars that suit him, as animals do. He is capable of recognizing particulars for what they are, i.e., a good, a partial realization of the good, and he is able to act accordingly." W. Van derMarck, "Ethics as a Key

to Aquinas' Theology, The Significance of Specification by Object," *Thomist* Vol. 40 (1976), p. 540.

31. In his cited Introduction, D'Arcy criticizes the dualism of the Rationalists. Yet he later writes, of translating *passio*, "perhaps the English word that would best hit the point is *reaction:* activity, yes, but an activity that is produced by some other agent: as Corvez renders it in French, *acte recu*" (p. xxii). Reid in his Appendix I seems more sensitive to the interplay between subject and object, but his language also betrays the Cartesian cant: "The terms emotion and motive both suggest an arousal or upsurge of psychic energy together with a reaction defined by the nature of an impinging stimulus" (p. 140).

32. Cf. *Quaes. Disp. De Ver.*, 22.12, and throughout his treatment of *appetitus*. Recall also the two modes of perfectibility for a creature.

33. Thus will and the appetible are in *communion,* but not "properly the communion of *form* (though that is presupposed). They are in a typically different communion in which each member stands *in its own mode of being* (the proper mode of communion of agent and patient)." Dewan, "The Real Distinction between Intellect and Will," p. 573, n. 36.

4. The Treatise on the Passions

1. I-II.22-48. Since most of the references in this chapter will be to that *Treatise,* I will only give the reference beginning with the Question.

2. I have translated "aliud" as "alien," since it fits the sense of a thing being drawn away from what is most fitting.

3. Note the force of *secundum* in "secundum transmutationem corporalem." It is difficult to translate exactly but the sense is certainly not "followed by" or even "accompanied by," though the latter is closer on the conceptual map. The sense is: "*according as there is* bodily transmutation." Cf. also 23.3, where Aquinas uses "ubi est."

God and the angels do not have passions, properly speaking (22.3ad3), not only because they do not have bodies which can undergo "transmutatio corporalis," but also, because they do not *need* passions to have their [recalcitrant] physicality *moved* toward attainment of the good. Cf. 24.3ad2; 31.4ad2.

4. The body, then, is a kind of "translation point" of the passivity and activity of the self. Again we discover Thomas' sense of organic unity, and of being a "moved mover," since Thomas believes that "Action and passion are a single act." Aquinas, *In Physic.*, lect. 8. Cf. Aristotle, *Physics,* V. 4. 228a20.

5. 21.1; see also 22.2. The reader of Latin should also pay attention to Aquinas' considered use of the passive voice throughout the *Treatise.*

6. The rational power of understanding works not directly, but through making a representation of a thing (*intentionem rei*).

7. He will eventually say that the lemonade has given *specificity* to your thirst (30.2; 43.1). In other words, you were generally thirsty, but when the lemonade was offered, it drew you in your thirstiness to it. So now you want *this glass* of lemonade.

8. André Combes attends to this progressive empowerment in "Le problème de la liberté d'après St. Thomas," *Divinitas* Vol. 18 (1974), p. 111.

9. That is why he cannot have "real union" with an object pole which is evil, because as evil it would be essentially *privative,* and, as depriving the subject pole of *motion*, actually deprives it of passion. Correspondingly, that is why the irascible passion of *anger* can have no opposite (23.3). Because every being has *some* good, some joy is possible even in pain (35.4).

10. The other is apprehended by the entire self, but using different [passive] powers of receptivity (I.79.6); see also 23.1.

11. Thomas' word for that is *conveniens*. Actually, the word means "coming together." That is a convenient translation if one is trying, as I am, to demonstrate that Thomas is speaking about interaction between self and other in the *Treatise.* I will continue to translate it as "fitting," with an overtone of "things coming together and 'fitting.'"

12. Mark D. Jones points out that "Thomas knew that his readers, being students of theology, have already been passionately converted by the Gospel." "Aquinas's Construction of a Moral Account of the Passions," *Freiburger Zeitschrift für Philosophie*

und Theologie, Vol. 33, Nos. 1-2 (1986), p. 97. This work is valuable for its tracing of Thomas' sources for his treatment of the passions.

13. Again, recall that all things that have being are good. That is also why "fitting" is a better translation than "right" (as in right or wrong).

14 . Early in the same *Responsio,* he uses the word "coaptio" three different times in three different forms. Thomas' use of the prefix "co(n)-", employed here and throughout the *Treatise* when seemingly unnecessary, lends linguistic weight to my claim that Thomas consistently intends to consider passions as a feature of *interaction* between object and subject poles in the *Treatise.* Note, finally, the phrase "through the love of God *(per amorem Dei)*": is this subjective or objective genitive? I believe that Thomas intended this ambiguity, since he wants to have it mean both at the same time.

15. Again, the indeterminacy of the genitive (subjective or objective) here is deliberate. Who is enjoying whom? Is God enjoying the human being or is the human being enjoying God? Both. See note #14.

16. The Latin word is *quies,* which D'Arcy, after a most illuminating discussion in his Introduction, suggests would best be translated as "pure play."

17. See 25.3, where Thomas is speaking of rationality permeating the entire human composite, even the passions. We must take such a statement in the light of what he means by rationality: delighting in the final goal of communion with God.

18. He means this the same way that Ekman uses "primary facial expressions"—except that Thomas wants it to refer to all activity of the passions, including all the "bodily transmutations."

19. The *Blackfriars* translation of that word is "overflow" or "spill over" (30.1ad1). That seems adequate, especially because of the root, "wave," which connotes water. The problem is that the use of the word "overflow" seems to imply that one event follows another temporally: first the movement of the intellect, then the rest of the self. That, in turn, subtly reinforces the concept that the intellect "acts upon" the rest of the person, as though it were an "exter-

nal force." It seems to underwrite the inadequate Cognitivist model of Perception-Appraisal-Action.

20. The problem, as we recall from Chapter 1, is with "immediate" and "automatic" appraisal (from the scientific point of view), and with ignoring the role of dispositions and habits (from the philosophical point of view), as we have seen in Chapter 2. Other Latin words contribute to that understanding of simultaneity. See note #24.

21. Still, Thomas will not admit of direct action between spirit and body (precisely because this would yield the "spirit in the machine" model), and so posits that the "middle" of the composite is the heart; cf. 24.2ad2; 37.4; and *De Veritate*, 26.8. Alternatively, he suggests that the "middle" of the composite is the "imagination." Thus he displays now a more physical, now a more intellectual, leaning in describing the operation of the composite.

22. Cf. also 35.1ad1; 37.1; 38.5ad3; and especially 45.2, where the "warming of the heart repels fear and causes hope"! We cannot imagine a more profound identification between "bodily transmutations" and passions. D'Arcy, the *Blackfriars* translator, is unable to translate this passage (38.5ad3) adequately. He puts it, "Every satisfactory bodily condition *does something for* the heart...." A reading of D'Arcy's translation will show how committed he is to the Cartesian model of control of the passions. This creates problems for him in the whole translation. Reid observes, "What is remarkable, given the limitations of time and opportunity, is St. Thomas' continuing interest in the role of bodily *resonance* in man's emotional life and the extent and diversity of his comments on the subject." App. VI, p. 172. Emphasis added.

23. The translator notes, "In the scholastics' incomplete stock analysis of causal explanation, and of substance-accident relations, there was simply no linguistic or conceptual apparatus available to express his profound and original understanding of the relation of the soul and its powers. Hence Thomas chose a term, 'resultance,' which evaded the hard-and-fast categories." The translation and note is from Timothy Suttor, translator and commentator, Vol. 11 of *Blackfriars*, (I.75-83), pp. 112-113, n. a. Cf. also 31.2ad1.

24. 24.4. When Thomas describes the way the lower *appetitus* follows (*con-sequens*) the higher *appetitus* in 30.1ad1, he uses the words resonates (*redundantia*) together with the word *simul* (simultane-

ously). The whole self is engaged simultaneously in the intellect's relationship with the other that is fitting for (attuned with) it.

25. Thomas' word here is *appetibile,* but for reasons that will soon be apparent, we need to render it "desirable" here.

26. I include "mutual" in the translation because we find here and throughout the *Treatise* a constant, consistent use of the prefix "co- ("con-", "com-"), which means "together with." Thomas uses that prefix in places where he would not seem to need it. Here, for example, we see it both in the words "com-placentia" ("mutual pleasure," "pleasure together with"), and "co-aptatione" ("co-apti-tude," "fitting together with").

27. Friendship is the best way to have passions, and even the form of all the virtues. It is how Thomas describes *agape,* charity: "friend-ship with God." The best discussion of this is Paul Wadell, *Friendship and the Moral Life* (Notre Dame: University of Notre Dame, 1989).

28. 26.2. His explanation of the motion there is at first a bit mystifying, but once we understand his problem, the passage becomes clear. Thomas wants to describe the give-and-take (circular) motion of interaction, and make it a part of the *Summa*'s overall (linear) motion of the return of the creature to God.

29. Cf. 27.4ad1&ad2, for a discussion of how *delectatio* (delight) char-acterizes the entire *appetitus* movement toward union. See 31:1 for a discussion of the transformation that continues during the union.

30. Cf. also 48.2. One of Aquinas' main concerns in QQ. 40-48 is to display the "sudden" bodily transmutations of specific passions, as "rational" *and* "rationalizable") in that they are already "ordered" toward approach or avoidance, acquisition or resistance *and* need to be fully rational to attain their end. Hence, for example, the *tremor* (trembling) of the bold occurs because of a "recalling of heat from the exterior to the interior." The result is a coldness in the body, from which we shiver, but also a "gathering of strength around the heart" so as to offer a burst of resistance to the object-to-be-avoided (45.4ad1).

31. For example, P. Kutter, *Die Menschlichen Leidenschaften* (Stuttgart-Berlin: Kreuzverlag, 1978), p. 43. Judith Barad admirably emphasizes the integration of the agent, but makes a

similar mistake on the supposed moral neutrality of emotions in "Aquinas on Emotions and Morals," *The Thomist*, Vol. 55, No. 3 (July 1991), p. 403, since she has an insufficient account of the richness of the subject-object interrelationship in Aquinas.

32. D'Arcy does translate *subjacent imperio rationis* as "subject to the control of reason." This is adequate, but simply insensitive to Aquinas' understanding of the rich relationship between reason and passion, which I hope to show now.

33. Jones, in "Aquinas's Construction of a Moral Account of the Passions," does a creditable job of delineating Thomas' understanding of "the governance of reason." However, his grammar is insistently one of "control" (93, 96, 97), and he seems to imply that this "quasi-political dominion of reason over the passions" (93) is paradigmatic for Thomas' whole treatment of rational passions. Romanus Cessario, O.P., *The Moral Virtues and Theological Ethics* (Notre Dame: University of Notre Dame Press, 1991), is aware that human passions are ordered toward right reason (64), but seems chiefly concerned with how we might exercise the rule of reason over disordered emotions.

34. That is, thinking of the passions in this way enables us to consider the "commonality" of passions, as shared with the sensate world. Jean Porter, in her *Recovery of Virtue* (Notre Dame: University of Notre Dame Press, 1990), p. 42, speaks also of the community of all species, but has missed the interaction among beings, and the fact that the human is a higher level of organization among beings.

35. Cf. I-II.50.3a1 and 34.1. Thus Thomas can say in 24.1a2, "even the lower appetitive powers are said to be rational, in that they also participate somehow in reason."

36. Discussed in the entire question 30, but especially see 30.3ad2.

37. Note how D'Arcy in 24.2 and throughout the *Treatise on the Passions* translates all of Thomas' metaphors, such as *limites rationes, moderatione rationis,* and *ordinatae a ratione* as "under rational control." In 24.3, he translates *conveniunt* as "under rational control."

38. Thomas must yield that one cannot love something without knowing it, but accounts for *natural* love (e.g. gravity) by cognition instilled by the Creator. This is, assuredly, the weakest "cognition" claimable.

39. In fact, Thomas etymologically relates the word *delectatio* (delight) to *electatio* (choice).

40. Thomas uses the same word, *quies*, about the final goal in 25.2; 26.2. He is once again insisting on the composite nature of the human being, and on her "bestriding" of the eternal and temporal worlds.

41. 32.3. Cf. 32.3ad3, and especially 37.4.

42. For that reason, Thomas says in 43.1, that an object pole can be *caused* by a subject pole. Humans (who have knowledge of God's plan) can also be said to "cause" objects because of the *purpose* they give to objects, since "having a purpose" is part of what makes an object to be what it is. Therefore, not only do we need objects to complete ourselves, objects need humans to complete them. So, in reality, there *are no* objects without subjects, or subjects without objects (though we can mentally make the distinction for the sake of discussion). A totally interactive model.

43. See 30.3a3. Cf. also I.78.4; I.81.3.

44. Cf. 35.2 and 37.4 for the human life described as a "motion which proceeds from the heart to the rest of the members of the body." In extreme cases, irascible passions can terminate life by terminating this motion; cf. 48.4ad3.

45. 35.2ad3. There, D'Arcy translates *gaudio animali* as "spiritual joy," completely missing Thomas' point: that joy "emerges" from *sensate* delight.

46. 39.1, "Sed Contra." Cf. also 39.2. Thomas uses "delight" when we would expect him, in his parallel schema, to use "joy." But it is simply impossible for Thomas to posit joy in evil.

47. In an insightful work, Wilkie Au notes, "While our own efforts are important and can bring about a certain feeling of wholeness, at times they, like the hasid's asceticism, will ultimately not achieve the permanent unity we desire. That unity will arrive gratuitously from the hand of God only after a lifetime of effort on our part." *By Way of the Heart: Toward a Holistic Christian Spirituality* (Mahwah: Paulist Press, 1989). Here, Au is attentive to the two notions of striving and surrender, but seems to think of them as sequential.

48. 39.2. Cf. 39.4: A will unable to discern evil is the most evil thing.

5. A Passion for God: *The Spiritual Exercises* of Ignatius of Loyola

1. Dictated to Luis Gonçalves da Câmara beginning in 1553, and ending, because of interruptions, in 1555. The text used here is Joseph F. O'Callaghan, trans., *The Autobiography of St. Ignatius Loyola* (New York: Harper & Row, 1974), hereafter referred to as *Auto.* This briefest of biographical sketches is taken from the Introduction to that work. The main source of reference for the life of Ignatius is the *Fontes Narrativi de S. Ignatio de Loyola*, 4 vols. (Rome, 1943-65), containing his own works, and those of his biographers. The *Fontes Narrativi* [hereafter referred to as *FN*] is, in turn, part of the *Monumenta Historica Societatis Jesu*, 124 vols. (Madrid and Rome, 1894–present), hereafter cited as *MHSJ*. For the most recent and comprehensive presentation of the historical sources for the life of Ignatius, cf. Paul Begheyn, S.J. and Kenneth Bogart, S.J., "A Bibliography on St. Ignatius's *Spiritual Exercises,*" *Studies in the Spirituality of Jesuits*, May 1991, Vol. 23/3. The authors have compiled 750 references under twenty-seven headings.

2. The Autograph, and various editions, including Latin translations, are presented in the *MHSJ,* Vol. 100. I have relied on my own translation of the text, supplemented by David L. Fleming, S.J., *The Spiritual Exercises of St. Ignatius, a Literal Translation and a Contemporary Reading* (St. Louis: Institute of Jesuit Sources, 1978); W.H. Longridge, *The Spiritual Exercises of St. Ignatius of Loyola, with a Commentary and a Translation of the Directorium in Exercitia* (London: A.R. Mowbray & Co., Ltd.), hereafter cited as Longridge; Louis J. Puhl, *The Spiritual Exercises of St. Ignatius, Based on Studies in the Language of the Autograph* (Chicago: Loyola University Press, 1951), hereafter cited as Puhl; and *Ignatius of Loyola: The Spiritual Exercises and Selected Works*, ed. by George E. Ganss, S.J. (Mahwah: Paulist Press, 1991), pp. 121-241, hereafter cited as Ganss, *SE.* I will use the standard numbering of the paragraphs of the *Exercises* and, when using another's translation, will cite the name. In addition, I have used the *Directory* (*Dir.*) commissioned by Acquaviva and com-

pleted in 1599 which is the first official instruction to accompany the *Spiritual Exercises* (*MHSJ,* Vol. 76, pp. 562ff).

3. Robert L. Schmitt, S.J., "The Christ-Experience and Relationship Fostered in the Spiritual Exercises of St. Ignatius of Loyola," *Studies in the Spirituality of Jesuits* (October 1974), p. 219. He states: "By encounter I mean a direct confrontation or meeting of another person at a deeply personal level in such a way that one is changed...."

4. It is interesting to note the number of times the *Exercises* use Spanish derivatives of the Latin *quies*. Cf. *SE,* 29, 35, 315 a), 315 b), 316, 317, etc.

5. Ignatius uses the Spanish *salvar su ánima* ("to save one's soul") here, but it is important to translate the word *ánima* (soul) correctly from the start. "I translate Ignatius' *ánima* by 'person' rather than 'soul.' Ignatius did not have a Platonic or Cartesian notion of man; he uses *ánima* merely in the figurative sense of taking the part for the whole." Jules Toner, *A Commentary on St. Ignatius' Rules for the Discernment of Spirits* (St. Louis: The Institute of Jesuit Sources, 1982), p. 24, n. 6. I ascribe to this synechdochical use of the word *ánima* as well, but wish to point out that the use of *that* part for the whole lends a special coloring to Ignatius' understanding of the human person. Cf. Ganss' comment on p. 77 in his translation of Ignatius' *Constitutions of the Society of Jesus* (St. Louis: The Institute of Jesuit Sources, 1970), and Ganss, *SE,* p. 392, n. 16.

6. This is a point about human nature which Hardon fails to emphasize clearly in his "Ignatian Spirituality Today," *Listening: Journal of Religion and Culture,* Vol. 26, No. 3, Fall 1991, p. 201.

7. Karl Rahner brings out another dimension of the meditation on the sin of the angels: that even "pure spirit" can sin. We are tempted to locate sin in the material—perhaps even the sexual—but the sin of "pure spirit" displays the falseness of such evaluation. *Betrachtungen zum ignatianischen Exerzitienbuch* (München: Kosel-Verlag, 1965), p. 50.

8. Philip S. Keane, S.S., *Christian Ethics and Imagination* (New York: Paulist Press, 1984), pp. 87-88. William F. Lynch, S.J., offers a similarly inclusive definition in *Christ and Prometheus: A*

New Image of the Secular (Notre Dame: University of Notre Dame Press, 1970), p. 23.

9. Edward Schillebeekx presents us with this insight into our relationship with Jesus in *Christ the Sacrament of the Encounter with God*, trans. by Mark Schoof and Laurence Bright (Kansas City: Sheed and Ward, 1963).

10. Sheldrake writes, "For God, all is eternally 'now,' and therefore it follows that I can speak to him as present not merely in the imagination but in reality.... The significance is a person, Jesus Christ, who is re-presented through the imaginative process. We are not, therefore, talking about going back in time in prayer, but entering rather into the eternal present." Philip Sheldrake, "Imagination and Prayer," *The Way* (1984), p. 99.

11. Jerome Nadal, contemporary and companion of Ignatius, emphasizes the importance of these two meditations in *MHSJ*, Vol. 66, p. 307.

12. *SE*, 95, 1. The Spanish "fused" wording portrays this intimacy better: "por tanto quien quisiere venir *conmigo* ha de trabajar *conmigo*, porque *siguiéndome* en la pena, también *me siga* en la gloria."

13. He uses that "sense-image," and then submits, "On the theological level this reality and the threat to it have been traditionally discussed in terms of 'the salvation of the soul.'" *Images of Hope* (Baltimore: Helicon Press, 1965), p. 212.

14. *Ibid.*, p. 49.

15. *SE*, 314. This is not to claim, of course, that mental illness is caused by evil spirits. But the dynamisms of depression can certainly be exacerbated by the evil spirit, and Lynch and others have discovered that the Rules for the Discernment of Spirits are extraordinarily helpful for leading one out of mental illness.

16. Ignatius' description of consolations (316) and desolations (317) takes up many of the themes we have already seen in Thomas. He states clearly that it is *not in our own power* to attain consolation (322), which can only be granted by God.

17. Cf. *Auto.* p. 24. After founding the Society of Jesus, Ignatius was discerning about the poverty of the newly formed order. He records his prayer experiences in his *Spiritual Journal* (henceforth cited as *Journal*) [*MHSJ Const.* I; trans. by William J. Young in *Woodstock Letters,* Vol. 87 (July 1958), 195-267]. In it we see the

extraordinary emphasis that Ignatius puts on tears in his discernment of God's will. The Second Part of the *Journal,* which encompasses nearly a year of prayer, is little more than a record of *whether or not he wept in prayer.* A deeper reading of the *Exercises,* and a greater attention to Ignatius' life and letters, would surely help to dispel a persistent misconception that Ignatian spirituality is finally one of rationality over against passion. See, for example, Sidney Callahan, *In Good Conscience: Reason and Emotion in Moral Decision Making* (San Francisco: Harper, 1991), who quotes Ignatius out of context and negatively on passions (p. 97).

18. This will eventually flower into the devotion to the body of Christ in the eucharist, and the body of Christ that is the church.

19. See *SE,* 89. For the historical importance of the individual's personal assent to God, see Fridolin Marxer, "Mystique ignatienne de la création et éducation de la foi," *Cahiers de spiritualité ignatienne,* Vol. 5 (1981), p. 241. For the significance of the body in this relationship, see Étienne Lepers, "L'application des sens, Exercices n. 121-126," *Christus,* Vol. 27 (1980), p. 91.

20. Cf. 15, 17, etc. "The term that appears most often as the norm of discernment is *conveniente.* The word signifies useful, suitable or conformable." John Futrell, *Making an Apostolic Community of Love* (St. Louis: Institute of Jesuit Sources, 1970), p. 117.

21. *SE,* 316. Note also the emphasis on *joy [leticia]* which Aquinas says that only human beings can experience; on "being drawn" *[llama y atrae]* which echoes the "receptivity" of "being moved" which is so crucial for Thomas' *Treatise on the Passions.*

22. Marie-Luce Brun, "Le corps...cet ami," *Cahiers de spiritualité ignatienne,* Vol. 6, No. 24 (Oct.–Déc. 1982), p. 237. Translation mine. Cf. Heb 4:12. Thus Coventry errs (and with him many "popular" interpreters of Ignatius) when he writes of this meditation, "Even apart from the somewhat lurid details, the soul-body dichotomy, which entered deep into Christian spirituality, is not compatible with our understanding of the incarnation, the redemption of the world, the *milieu divin,* the building of the kingdom on earth." John Coventry, "Sixteenth and Twentieth Century Theologies of Sin," *The Way, Supplement,* Vol. 48 (Autumn 1983), p. 57.

23. For a discussion of this movement, see Werner Löser, "Konturen ignatianischer Spiritualität; Zur Exerzitienbetrachtung 'um Liebe zu erlangen'," *Geist und Leben,* Vol. 51 (1978), p. 265. Cf. also Marxer, "Mystique ignatienne…" p. 237.

24. Charmot suggests that the participant "clothes herself" with the very same compassion for the world that Christ had, in F. Charmot, *L'Union au Christ dans L'Action selon saint Ignace* (Paris: Bonne Presse, 1959), p. 197.

25. Ignatius allows great freedom to the individual in her imagining of the scene, whether it is "narrow or broad or level" (192). Ignatius himself had been to the holy land, and could easily have described the place for the retreatant, but in allowing the summoning up of the retreatant's *own* sense of place, we notice again the importance of the individual's unique and particular engagement with Jesus.

26. Charles Viard, "Le lie de la compassion. La troisième semaine d'Exercices spirituels," *Christus,* Vol. 28 (1981), pp. 362, 368. Translation mine.

27. Cf. *SE,* 87, on penances, and especially, 157: If the participant has a repugnance to poverty, which he knows is "disordered," not "right" (because it is not "like Christ"), then he is instead to "wish, seek and supplicate for it."

28. The participant's "appropriate" distress and gratitude is increased by that knowledge, as the *Directory* tells us, that "each ought to look upon himself as though he were in truth the cause of all the immense sufferings and humiliations which the Son of God endured, and then to consider that whatever of spiritual good and gifts of grace he enjoys, his deliverance from eternal woe, and his hope of obtaining eternal happiness, all have come to him from the merits of Christ; and indeed that Christ, while he suffered, had before His eyes both us and all our sins one by one, and prayed for us, and obtained for us forgiveness and grace." XXXV, 3 (Longridge, p. 387).

29. B. Schellenberger, "Gottes Mit-Leid mit uns Menschen," *Geist und Leben,* Vol. 49, (1976), p. 402. Translation mine. Cf. *Dir.,* XXXV, 4-9, for the proper attitudes and thoughts for the participant during this time. "…one should recognize and venerate the infinite wisdom and goodness of God, which devised so suitable a means for *melting the hearts* of men and *drawing them to Himself by His*

love.... Fourthly, and chiefly, our *love for God is inflamed* by the *consideration* of such great goodness.... Lastly, we may and ought to conceive a great zeal for souls, seeing that God has valued them so highly and loved them with so great a love, and bought them at so great a price." Emphasis added.

30. Cf. *Auto.* p. 47. Leo Bakker states that Ignatius expects Christ to appear to the participant to console him, and to place two alternatives before him—spiritual or literal imitation, in *Freiheit und Erfahrung* (Würzburg, 1970); see pp. 82, 255. I have often found, while directing retreats, that Christ appears to one of my directees.

31. I should point out that those who come from abusive homes must be directed very carefully during this week. There is a profound tendency to identify abuse as "the will of God" in many cases, and to see God, perhaps, as the abusive parent. While being open to the action of the Holy Spirit, it is good for the director to stress how Jesus identifies with the abused person here, and enters into the abusive situation precisely to rescue and liberate him or her, "to convict the world of sin," and to establish justice. It is also common for many other experiences of personal grief and loss to be evoked during this week. The director should be sensitive to all of this.

32. Young experiences a similar difficulty in translating a section of Ignatius' *Journal,* for Ignatius writes, "After retiring I felt a special consolation in thinking of Them [the Three Persons of the Blessed Trinity] *embracing me* with interior rejoicing in my soul and then falling to sleep." To that, Young appends this note: "It is not clear whether Ignatius is speaking of embracing himself, or of an embrace by the Three Persons." *Journal,* pp. 214-215. Emphasis added.

33. Again, the Spanish is unclear whether this *con mucho afecto* refers to God's giving, or to my receiving, the gifts.

34. *SE*, 234. Note again the effect of the "fusion of words" in the Spanish, articulating the continuity of God and his gifts, and the deep mutuality between the Lord and the participant.

35. "...Ignatian 'will' is not identified with willing, but with human affectivity." Jacques Lewis, "La connaissance spirituelle dans les Exercices," *Cahiers de spiritualité ignatienne,* Vol. 5, No. 20 (July–September 1981), p. 178. Translation mine.

36. *SE*, 234. Emphasis added. He then suggests that the well-known "Take and Receive" prayer be said "with as much affection as possible."

37. Haas argues persuasively from various Ignatian texts and letters that the God to be found in all things is Christ. Adolf Haas, "The Mysticism of St. Ignatius according to His *Spiritual Diary*," esp. pp. 196-199. Cf. also Parmananda Divarkar, *Alive to God* (Anand, India: X. Diaz del Rio, 1979), especially p. 7.

6. A Passion for Justice

1. Rosemary Radford Ruether, *Sexism and God-Talk. Toward a Feminist Theology* (Boston: Beacon Press, 1983), p. 30.

2. Anthony DePalma, "10-Year-Old Boy Is Charged as Adult In Fatal Shooting of 7-Year-Old Girl," *The New York Times*, August 26, 1989, p. 6:1. The final disposition of the case was reported in *The New York Times*, September 3, 1992, "13-Year-Old Pleads No Contest in Killing of Friend," p. A16:4. The boy was convicted of misdemeanor involuntary manslaughter and placed on probation until he is twenty-one. The family can have no weapons at home, and the boy cannot have a gun, until the boy is twenty-one.

3. Philip Shenon, "War Cries and Whistling in the Dark," *The New York Times*, February 4, 1991, p. A9.

4. Terry Leonard, AP, "As She Waits to Kill, Bosnian Recalls Peace," *The Boston Globe*, July 1, 1992, p. 12.

5. Robert Jay Lifton, *The Future of Immortality, and Other Essays for a Nuclear Age* (New York: Basic Books, 1987), p. 197.

6. Interview in *Sports Illustrated*, August 28, 1989, p. 56.

7. "Interview: Peter Hagelstein," *Omni Magazine*, May 1989, p. 78.

8. *Ibid.*, p. 94.

9. Deborah Prothrow-Stith, with Michaele Weissman, *Deadly Consequences* (New York: HarperCollins, 1991), p. 14. Not only does Prothrow-Stith analyze the phenomenon of violence from a public health perspective, but she offers, and has instituted, educational programs for conflict resolution. It is therefore one of the most hopeful and constructive books on U.S. violence I have ever read.

10. Elizabeth Schüssler Fiorenza, *In Memory of Her. A Feminist Theological Reconstruction of Christian Origins* (New York: Crossroad, 1983), pp. 256-257. Her entire chapter 7, "Christian Mission and the Patriarchal Order of the Household," pp. 251-284, is instructive in revealing the misogyny of western philosophy.

11. *Sexism and God-Talk*, p. 26.

12. Audre Lorde, *Sister Outsider* (Freedom: The Crossing Press, 1984), p. 39.

13. Thus to prepare us for her statement that *"Love is passionate,"* and bonding, Carter Heyward first points out that "our sexuality is our desire to participate in making love, making justice, in the world.... Where there is not justice—between two people or among thousands—there is no love. And where there is no justice/no love, sexuality is perverted into violence and violation...." *Our Passion for Justice, Images of Power, Sexuality and Liberation* (New York: Pilgrim Press, 1984), p. 86.

14. Melissa Everett, *Breaking Ranks* (Philadelphia: New Society Publishers, 1989), p. 24.

15. Mohandas K. Gandhi, *Young India,* October 8, 1925. Quoted in *The Essential Gandhi. An Anthology of His Writings on His Life, Work and Ideas,* ed. by Louis Fischer (New York: Vintage Books, 1983), p. 199. See also his *Hind Swaraj or Indian Home Rule* (Ahmedabad: Navajivin Publishing House, 1938), pp. 57-58.

16. In a speech at Emory University on April 22, 1988.

17. Carter Heyward's address, "Till Now We Had Not Touched Our Strength" (*Our Passion for Justice,* pp. 123-131), is particularly insightful on the religious dynamics behind the acquiescence to violence, and on the necessity for love "which is just, mutually empowering, and co-creative" (p. 124).

18. Cf. I-II.46.2,4,6.

19. J. Giles Milhaven, *Good Anger* (Kansas City: Sheed and Ward, 1989), p. 79, emphasis added. Especially in chapters 5 and 8 Milhaven studies this passion for justice in Thomas.

20. Take, for example, Milhaven's statement, "We felt deep satisfaction when the Massada [sic: Mossad] finally killed on the street the man who had masterminded the massacre of Jewish athletes at Munich. We felt this satisfaction even if we had little hope it would discourage Arabs from future terrorism" (87). Though

many Arabs have come to expect the terrible racist stereotyping of Milhaven's second sentence, it is useful to note it, since it grounds the "satisfaction" that Milhaven claims "we" felt at the Mossad assassination. If we were to examine the story from the Palestinian point of view, then the Palestinians who killed the Israeli athletes could be seen as victims, asking their oppressors to "Take Me Seriously," to "Feel My Power! Feel My Pain!"—to use Milhaven's words. There is, in short, no attempt to consider the dehumanizing effect of violence on the other (or the self). In fact, Milhaven shows by his racist statement that embracing such dehumanization is necessary for such an acceptance of violence.

21. In *Young India*, August 11, 1920, quoted in Fischer, pp. 156-157.

22. I believe that Matthew is making the same point when he presents Jesus at the time of his arrest, as saying to Peter, "Put your sword back, for all who draw the sword will die by the sword. Or do you think that I cannot appeal to my Father, who would promptly send more than twelve legions of angels to my defense?" (26:53).

23. Carter Heyward, *Our Passion for Justice*, pp. 85 (emphasis in text), 87. Her major contribution, and thematic insight, is that "sexuality is a protest against structures of alienation. It is a NO! to humiliation; a NO! to the denial or the human—created and creative—yearning for reciprocal, mutually empowering connections" (p. 130).

24. Hauerwas is beginning his chapter on "Peacemaking" by commenting on the confrontation spoken of in Matthew 18:15-22, in *Christian Existence Today*, p. 90.

25. There are many studies of the success of the Filipino "EDSA" revolution which ousted Marcos in 1986. For the best study of the practice of Christian non-violence in the field, see Niall O'Brien, *Revolution from the Heart* (Maryknoll: Orbis, 1987, 1991).

26. Audre Lorde, *Sister Outsider*, p. 124.

27. One of the writers who best describes the benefits of this outcast community is Mary Daly, *Beyond God the Father. Toward a Philosophy of Women's Liberation* (Boston: Beacon Press, 1973). She tells that after a woman has the courage of facing non-being [i.e., dismissal from the patriarchal structures that had given her identity], she finds a dynamic and communal intuition of being (p. 32). She states that the "emergence of the communal vocational

self-awareness of women is a *creative political ontophany*" (34), since it exists on the boundaries of the patriarchal structure, destabilizing that structure while sharing life within its own community (55).

28. Stanley Hauerwas, *Against the Nations*, p. 16.
29. *Ibid.,* p. 117.
30. Stanley Hauerwas, *The Peaceable Kingdom. A Primer in Christian Ethics* (Notre Dame: University of Notre Dame Press, 1983), p. 45.
31. *Ibid.,* p. 76.
32. In a slightly different context, Aristotle recognized this in his *Nicomachean Ethics,* when he wrote that men of courage do not make the best professional soldiers (1117b).
33. Again, this "can't" is not a statement of physical impossibility, but of moral impossibility. We can't harm, because the anger has been so well integrated that to act upon it without having it governed by non-violent love would be to disintegrate the self, and rupture the paradigmatic relationship to God in Jesus.
34. "Letter to Diognetus," 7:4, *The Apostolic Fathers,* tr. by Kirsopp Lake, Vol. 2 (New York: Macmillan, 1913), p. 365.

INDEX

AUTHORS CITED IN TEXT